ROCKABYE

JOANNA MURRAY-SMITH

Currency Press,
Sydney

CURRENCY PLAYS

First published in 2009
by Currency Press Pty Ltd,
PO Box 2287, Strawberry Hills, NSW, 2012, Australia
enquiries@currency.com.au
www.currency.com.au
in association with
Melbourne Theatre Company

NATIONAL LIBRARY OF AUSTRALIA CIP DATA

Author:	Murray-Smith, Joanna.
Title:	Rockabye / Joanna Murray-Smith.
ISBN:	9780868198606 (pbk.)
Series:	Current Theatre Series.
Other Authors / Contributors:	
	Melbourne Theatre Company.
Dewey Number:	A822.3

Contents

Typeset by Dean Nottle for Currency Press.
Printed by Hyde Park Press, Richmond, SA.
Cover image by Lydia Baic.
Cover design by Emma Vine, Currency Press.

To John Bluthal

Rockabye was first produced by Melbourne Theatre Company at The MTC Theatre, Sumner, Melbourne, on 8 August 2009, with the following cast:

SIDNEY JONES	Nicki Wendt
JULIA	Kate Atkinson
ALFIE / KURT	Richard Piper
TOBIAS BERESFORD	Pacharo Mzembe
LAYLA	Zahra Newman
ESME	Betty Bobbitt
JOLYON	Daniel Frederiksen

Director, Simon Phillips
Set Designer, Brian Thomson
Costume Designer, Esther Marie Hayes
Lighting Designer, Philip Lethlean
Composer / Sound Designer, Peter Farnan

CHARACTERS

SIDNEY JONES, attractive, slim, 40s
JULIA, late 20s/early 30s, very attractive
ALFIE, in his late 40s/early 50s
TOBIAS BERESFORD, around 30, handsome, black
LAYLA, around 30, beautiful, black
ESME, in her 60s
JOLYON, in his 30s
KURT, in his 30s, German

The actor who plays Jolyon or Alfie can also play Kurt.

ACKNOWLEDGMENTS

My thanks go to Matt Cameron, Peter Farnan, Raymond Gill and the cast of the Melbourne Theatre Company production for their invaluable insights in the evolution of the play. Thanks also to Ann Tonks, Kylie McCormack, Martina Murray and all at the MTC. Particular thanks to Simon Phillips, for endurance, insight, patience, fortitude and faith.

This play went to press before the end of rehearsals and may differ from the play as performed.

OPENING IMAGE

A spotlight in the middle of darkness. A roughly constructed, makeshift bassinet with a baby in it. A soundscape builds. It's the soundtrack of a life—tiny snatches of African music, crying, laughter, a mother singing a lullaby, traffic noises, animal noises, babies crying, soothing words, airplane noises, snatches of conversation, more African music, lullabies, TV, radio—a chaotic but rhythmically beautiful jumble of culturally diverse sounds, stolen from a life.

The spotlight diminishes on the bassinet, which vanishes, as the lights come up.

SCENE ONE

An elegant, hiply decorated London mansion.

SIDNEY, *a very attractive, thin woman in her mid forties, wearing expensive exercise clothes, is sitting on a sofa in a smartly appointed home office with her feet on the coffee table while* JULIA, *casually dressed, wearing a Bluetooth and carrying a clipboard, stands in front of her.*

Their exchange is rapid-fire.

SIDNEY: And the thing—
JULIA: Done—
SIDNEY: The benefit—
JULIA: I said no—
SIDNEY: Nicely?
JULIA: Very nicely—You've previously—
SIDNEY: Yes, I have—
JULIA: Committed to a—
SIDNEY: What?
JULIA: Breast—
SIDNEY: Good—

JULIA: Cancer—
SIDNEY: Excellent—
JULIA: Function previously—
SIDNEY: Good—
JULIA: Previous to their own.

Quick beat.

SIDNEY: *Is* there a breast cancer function?
JULIA: No.

Quick beat.

SIDNEY: Photos?
JULIA: They wanted the second one—
SIDNEY: The big—the one with—
JULIA: The muscly one—
SIDNEY: The big guy in the thong—
JULIA: In the thong, yes. Well—
SIDNEY: —endowed.
JULIA: Jamal—
SIDNEY: The one with me—
JULIA: He had his crotch in your—
SIDNEY: Where are we with the visa?
JULIA: Howard's onto it. The whole firm is—Howard cancelled the holiday—
SIDNEY: He cancelled a public holiday?
JULIA: Not for the public—
SIDNEY: He cancelled a public holiday?
JULIA: For the firm. You know he's always trying to impress you.
SIDNEY: Did I ask?
JULIA: No.
SIDNEY: Did I?
JULIA: No.
SIDNEY: For your opinion?
JULIA: No you didn't.
SIDNEY: Coloured tabs?

JULIA: They only make single colours.

SIDNEY: I *wanted* multicoloured.

JULIA: You can mix the packets yourself.

SIDNEY: What? *Self-mix?*

JULIA: Let's move on.

SIDNEY: The wheatgerm.

JULIA: Didn't have Peruvian. Only, ah, wherever it normally comes from.

SIDNEY: I have to do everything myself!

JULIA: I've got Esme on the net.

SIDNEY: Esme thinks the net is something you wear on your head at bedtime.

JULIA: I'm training her.

SIDNEY: It has to be Peruvian or I'm bloated—

JULIA: I know.

SIDNEY: The bloats—

JULIA: I know.

SIDNEY: And if that happens, the wardrobe's ruined.

JULIA: Berlin—

SIDNEY: Let's talk about Berlin—

JULIA: Berlin's good—

SIDNEY: Did you stop by?

JULIA: Yes

SIDNEY: And?

JULIA: They have the size six.

SIDNEY: Hallelujah!

JULIA: That's the good news.

SIDNEY: Slowly.

JULIA: The size six is missing a button.

SIDNEY: What?

JULIA: Yes—

SIDNEY: A button?

JULIA: Yes.

SIDNEY: You're kidding me?

JULIA: No. Unfortunately.
SIDNEY: Did they look?
JULIA: They looked.
SIDNEY: They looked?
JULIA: They had fifteen sales assistants on it.
SIDNEY: *Blind* sales assistants.
JULIA: They're looking but it's not simple.
SIDNEY: Haven't they got another fucking button?
JULIA: In Paris. Maybe. Only they'd have to actually make it.
SIDNEY: They'd have to make it?
JULIA: Somebody would have to make it. And not just anybody.
SIDNEY: The suspense is killing me.
JULIA: Yvette.
SIDNEY: Yvette?
JULIA: Makes that button.
SIDNEY: Yvette.
JULIA: The button maker. Apparently there are three women in the *atelier* and they make the buttons. But first they'd have to source the original fabric.
SIDNEY: Before they make the button?
JULIA: It's a silk crepe de chine.
SIDNEY: Do I look like an idiot?
JULIA: The fabric's no longer in the *atelier*, so they have to go to the source.
SIDNEY: The source.
JULIA: In the foothills.
SIDNEY: The foothills?
JULIA: The Uzbekistan foothills.
SIDNEY: They make fabric in the Uzbekistan foothills?
JULIA: Yes they do. And to make the button they have to send someone in—
SIDNEY: To Uzbekistan?
JULIA: To the underground city. The only way in is by mountain goat.
SIDNEY: To get a one-inch piece of ocelot-print crepe de chine?
JULIA: If you want the top—

SIDNEY: I want the top—
JULIA: You need the button.
SIDNEY: Who's got the goat?
JULIA: I'm on top of it—
SIDNEY: You're on top of the goat?
JULIA: Metaphorically.

Beat. They both sit in silence.

SIDNEY: Get the goat.
JULIA: Consider it… got. [*Beat.*] Okay. The Arbiter.
SIDNEY: [*steeling herself*] Okay.
JULIA: There's a chance.
SIDNEY: There's no chance, Julia.
JULIA: He might like it—
SIDNEY: He won't like it—
JULIA: Alfie sent over a file of his stuff. He wants you to read it just in case—
SIDNEY: What stuff?
JULIA: Everything from Lady Gaga to Angelina Jolie.
SIDNEY: He hates me, Julia—
JULIA: It's worth a shot. He's the one, Sidney.
SIDNEY: I know he's the one, Julia.
JULIA: He's the one who can—
SIDNEY: I know, Julia. I know he's the one.
JULIA: Only last week, he won a *British Press Award*—
SIDNEY: A *Hackademy* award, you mean—
JULIA: He's not a hack—
SIDNEY: They're all hacks, Julia—
JULIA: He's a very very well-respected hack, Sidney. And his late-night show is officially the hippest show in town.
SIDNEY: Oh, so *I*—an industry fixture with *decades* of—of—of success and many many award… nights—and three ads and at least one affair with European royalty, am expected to *prostrate* myself before a twenty-something upstart who happens to be riding the zeitgeist, in the hope that he deigns to shine his benevolent light on my new album?

Beat.

JULIA: Yes.

SIDNEY: [*just slightly hopeful*] He's heard the album?

JULIA: He's heard it—

SIDNEY: Jesus, Lord!

JULIA: Alfie's talking to him now.

Beat as they ponder the profundity of this thought.

Oh. She's arrived.

SIDNEY: [*a change of tack entirely*] She's here?

JULIA: In the sitting room.

SIDNEY: Why didn't you tell me?!

JULIA: I am telling you.

SIDNEY: Did Esme get her something to eat?

JULIA: She's not—

SIDNEY: Okay.

JULIA: She ate on the plane.

SIDNEY: Well, for God's sake tell her—

JULIA: I did. [*Beat.*] I was wondering if tonight—

SIDNEY: Oh, no—

JULIA: Tonight—

SIDNEY: Jesus!

JULIA: It's a wedding. Can I—?

SIDNEY: A wedding!

JULIA: Can I—?

SIDNEY: Is it *your* wedding?

JULIA: Well, no.

SIDNEY: Don't I pay you enough? Is your life so horrible? You know what's going on for me right now. You know how much support I need. And yet you still want to go to weddings, *like they matter*, like they're forever. Let me tell you something, in eight months he'll be bonking his travel agent and she'll be sick of the way he holds his cutlery.

JULIA: Oh.

SIDNEY: They'll be dividing up the Cristofle before you can say 'it'll never work'.

JULIA: They seem very much in love.

SIDNEY *snorts.*

Really.

SIDNEY: Love is just the gratitude you feel when you discover someone willing to indulge your self-delusions.

JULIA: My friend is getting married. I want to be happy for her.

SIDNEY: Well, that's the point, isn't it? From now on in, you're going to *have* to be happy for her, because *she's* never going to be happy again.

JULIA: My God!

SIDNEY: Go if you must. Just make sure you tell everyone how flexible I am. All your PA buddies. I know you gossip.

JULIA: We don't gossip.

SIDNEY: *Yes, you do, Julia.*

JULIA: So I can—

SIDNEY: Go. Go. Get lost. Get your hair done. And tell her I'll be there in minutes.

SCENE TWO

ALFIE *is Sidney's manager: fiftyish, hyperactive, loquacious, a self-made man, well-dressed, behind his desk. In front of the desk is* TOBIAS BERESFORD, *English of black African descent, Cambridge educated, middle-class, a journalist.*

Snappy:

ALFIE: I've always wanted to meet the face that launched a thousand profiles—

TOBIAS: Oh, I'm not—

ALFIE: You certainly are, my boy. You're the one. I always find myself—I'm reading and I'm thinking 'this is unusually accurate' and then I flick back and the by-line is invariably 'Tobias Beresford'. I've long thought I'd like to meet this man because *he knows his stuff* and—importantly—he's got style.

TOBIAS: Thanks.

ALFIE: Love the late-night show—

TOBIAS: Kind.

ALFIE: Last week you got six thousand Twitters, I believe—

TOBIAS: Love a good twitter.

ALFIE: Clever little show—

TOBIAS: Good team.

ALFIE: The way you pontificate would be pompous in anyone else, but you pull it off. Funky but authoritative.

TOBIAS: Do my best.

ALFIE: Congrats on the award.

TOBIAS: Silly. Awards.

ALFIE: Still.

TOBIAS: Still.

ALFIE: A thinker and a man who has a feeling for the pulse points of the people.

TOBIAS: Oh, no more fulsome flattery or I'll feel faint from alliteration!

ALFIE: See! That's what I'm talking about. Witty but… *educated.*

They smile. Beat.

Enjoyed your piece on Billie Gothic.

TOBIAS: Ta.

ALFIE: Not sure she warranted eighteen hundred words.

TOBIAS: Her star is rising.

ALFIE: You know she came to me for representation?

TOBIAS: She's with Helter Skelter—

ALFIE: I told her that I wasn't her man.

TOBIAS: Really?

ALFIE: Know her granny. Saw the potential—

TOBIAS: She's sixteen. She's hot.

ALFIE: She's hot. She's sixteen. But I wanted to give Sidney my full attention.

TOBIAS: It would be hard to give Sidney your full attention if you also had Billie Gothic.

ALFIE: Because she's hot.

TOBIAS: And sixteen.

ALFIE: But Sidney's my girl. [*Beat.*] I'll never forget the week *Supernova* went triple platinum. Do you remember, Tobias? There wasn't a talk show, radio host or print media that didn't want a piece of Sidney Jones.

TOBIAS: Er… I was a bit young.

ALFIE: 'Course you were. But by Christ she blew Whitney out of the water.

TOBIAS: Well done her!

ALFIE: Out of the fucking water. Kim Wilde, Shania, Sheena, Whitney, Siousxe Sioux. Katrina and the Waves. She had waves. But not wind as it turned out. Sidney blew them out of the water. She had *cred*—

TOBIAS: Not as much as Deborah Harry—

ALFIE: *Only* Deborah Harry—

TOBIAS: Or Sinead—

ALFIE: Let's leave out the nut-jobs—

TOBIAS: Madge—

ALFIE: 'What Am I Called?' is in *Rolling Stone*'s best top fifty pop anthems ever. Ever as in *ever*. As in, since the Middle Ages.

TOBIAS: She blew Joan of Arc out of the water too, then.

ALFIE: [*ignoring him*] Then she got the gig fronting Virginia Slims in Japan and we knew we'd hit the pinnacle.

TOBIAS: Briefly.

ALFIE: Oh, she was riding high for quite some time. *Supernova* went triple platinum in eight countries.

TOBIAS: Five number one hits in three years.

ALFIE: And four number twos and *sixteen* in Eastern Europe. She's officially been deemed a Living National Treasure in Minsk—

TOBIAS: Belarus?

ALFIE: You bet!

TOBIAS: But she's not Belarusian—

ALFIE: They had to widen the pool.

TOBIAS: Okay, but that was the mid eighties, Alfie. Since then she's been pretty much treading water artistically—

ALFIE: More than treading water, with respect—

TOBIAS: Dog paddling, then.

ALFIE: Certainly, there've been some tougher years.

TOBIAS: Dropped by Sony.

ALFIE: Dropped by Sony, but more recently picked up, my young friend, by MCA whose A and R guys, sorting the wheat from the riffraff, recognised an undeniable star. Perfectly poised for the comeback.

TOBIAS: Love to talk to her.

ALFIE: And you will, son. I know you're going to do the kind of profile that will resurrect the reputation of your chosen profession.

TOBIAS: As I said on the phone, I like the album.

ALFIE: [*everything hanging*] It's a serious album.

TOBIAS: It is a serious album. I'll be honest, it surprised me. It's emotional.

ALFIE: It's the real deal.

TOBIAS: I really didn't think… Well, to be honest, she's become a bit of a joke.

ALFIE: [*suddenly very serious*] She was never a joke.

TOBIAS: Alfie, with respect, she never really nailed the chameleonic thing. Time marched on and she stood still. But I have to say, the phoenix appears to be rising.

ALFIE: She knows who she is, Tobias, Toby. Can I call you Toby?

TOBIAS: No.

ALFIE: When people ask themselves that question 'who am I?', they are frequently forced to admit that they have no idea. In this album, Sidney asks that question and the question gets answered. 'I'm me.' That is what this album is about. It's about someone saying '*I'm me*'.

TOBIAS: Uh-huh.

ALFIE: I'm doing my best to get you an audience tomorrow before she heads to Berlin.

TOBIAS: I'm thinking the show and a major print profile, but I have to talk to her. Otherwise it would just be a puff piece—

ALFIE: Oh, we've got nothing at all against puff pieces—

TOBIAS: She deserves something better than that—

ALFIE: *Of course* she does.

TOBIAS: I'd like to go big on this, Alfie.

ALFIE: No such thing as too big.

TOBIAS: She's a survivor—

ALFIE: And for one very good reason. She's got it.

TOBIAS: She's got—

ALFIE: *It*. The thing. Always has. Virtuosic set of vocal chords and more charisma than the whole of Lichtenstein.

TOBIAS: I'd go further.

ALFIE: All right then, Malta. And even though she's pushing forty, she's *still* got it.

TOBIAS: I think she's pushed forty, actually, Alfie. Forty has fallen off the cliff. It's lying, fragmented, on the rocky shores of fifty.

ALFIE: Please don't mention that word—I'm phobic about it. The point is, it's all changed, Tobias. We've got sex kittens who in the old days would have been up to nine lives. Look at Helen Mirren—

TOBIAS: What about her?

ALFIE: Do-able.

TOBIAS: Speak for yourself—

ALFIE: Saw a photo on the weekend. Nigh on seventy and in a bikini on the Adriatic. Eminently do-able. Sidney just needs a teeny-weeny bit of rediscovery.

TOBIAS: I'm servicing my public, Alfie, not your marketing needs—

ALFIE: Of course you are, son. I can assure you that we fully understand the press thrives on freedom from influence, separation of church and state, cornerstone of a thriving, blah, blah. Totally on your side, matey. But that's the angle, no, my son? She's back. Firing on all cylinders.

TOBIAS: When she's going to crack the US, Alfie?

ALFIE: Let's start with the good news. She is enormous in Germany and Belgium and Croatia and Norway and Poland.

TOBIAS: I believe so.

ALFIE: Best-selling female artist of the year in Germany and Poland. She's on magazine covers every week in Poland. Makes the Minskis look tepid. She's a huge star in Poland. When she walks down a

Warsaw street, she is literally mobbed by Polish people. Many, many Polish people.

TOBIAS: And that's great.

Beat.

ALFIE: This record is special. Because you know what, Tobias, it's not just a piece of marketing chutzpah, throw in some big name producers, a couple of tracks with Justin or Nick Cave, whatever, and Bob's your uncle. No. Because that's not who she is, Tobias. She's an *artiste*—and they are regular pains in the *derrière* at times because they demand so much of themselves and in the course demand so much of those around them—but, my young friend, she is *the genuine article.*

TOBIAS: And I'd like to write a genuine article about the genuine article, if only I could talk to her.

ALFIE: I'd happily make a billion dollars from a piece of unadulterated shite sung by a buxom blonde sixteen-year-old because the world has no discernable standards, but that's not my Sid. That woman has dragged me kicking and screaming into the world of *integrity.* She's my passport. She's my visa application. She's changed me for the better. I'm being dragged along on the coat-tails of her lofty personal standards. It's hard, I can tell you, but I'm adapting. [*Beat. He smiles.*] This album is going to make her a serious somebody.

TOBIAS: Again.

ALFIE: Again.

SCENE THREE

LAYLA, *a beautiful black African woman, English-educated, middle-class, around thirty, is looking at the photographs of* SIDNEY *and famous people decorating the shelves in the sitting room, which is a perfect incarnation of contemporary, sophisticated, fashionable interior décor: modern art, chandeliers, Italian sofas. In front of her is a tray with two glasses and a bottle of Evian.*

SIDNEY *enters.*

LAYLA: Is that—no!

SIDNEY: Yes—

LAYLA: You and—

SIDNEY: Yes.

LAYLA: Holy—! Lordy. He looks—

SIDNEY: Oh, he's such an old sleaze, had his large nose in my cleavage, but she's fabulous—very funny—

LAYLA: True?

SIDNEY: A genuine wit and sexual charisma by the bucketload—

LAYLA: Seriously?

SIDNEY: Everyone thought it was Margaret who was the goer but both sisters drove the men wild with desire, I kid you not. Well of course, men do love a babe with a castle. I know from experience.

LAYLA: [*another photo*] And Posh!

SIDNEY: Before she turned into a surly-faced Ora-bronzed human whisk.

LAYLA: Oh!

SIDNEY: The only thing she's good for now is beating an omelette.

Beat. They survey each other a second then SIDNEY *crosses to her, extending a hand.*

Sidney.

Beat.

LAYLA: Layla.

SIDNEY: We didn't—?

LAYLA: No, I was in Harare that week.

SIDNEY: I was with that other guy—

LAYLA: He's out of the agency now, you were his last application—

SIDNEY: I finished him off!

LAYLA: Exactly!

SIDNEY: I have a reputation for finishing people off—

LAYLA: I know! Even in deepest, darkest—

SIDNEY: It's great that you're here.

LAYLA: Finally.

SIDNEY: They told me four months. That was six months ago—

LAYLA: That's actually not unusual. The documents all have to be certified and authenticated—

SIDNEY: I know—

LAYLA: Things get held up at the Protocol Office—

SIDNEY: I'm impatient! It's an Aries thing.

LAYLA: A date's been provisionally set for the hearing in May—

SIDNEY: Okay.

LAYLA: [*apologetically*] It's a process.

SIDNEY: Have you? Did Esme offer?

LAYLA: Thank you, yes.

SIDNEY: How was the flight?

LAYLA: Eleven hours.

SIDNEY: Pure hell. Unless you're in a private jet.

LAYLA: I've never been in a private jet.

SIDNEY: Oh, silly status symbols. Nothing to write home about.

LAYLA: I think I probably would—

SIDNEY: You think you would—?

LAYLA: Write home about it. You travel a lot, yeah?

SIDNEY: It's just like some boring club and every goddamn place you go, it's the same bunch of fabulous nobodies: Liz Hurley (gag!), Donatella, Marie-Celeste, Elle and her Birkin Bags. Christenings in Monte Carlo, summer rentals on Pantarella, wherever you go, someone's just been on Valentino's yacht and someone else is dating some Eurotrash financier, *like it matters*. To be honest, Layla, I'm sick of the pointless, mind-numbing wealth. I'm sick of the superficiality, the emptiness!

ESME, *sixty-something, well-groomed but with the unmistakable sense of having had a hard life, sticks her head in.*

ESME: Excuse me, but we've tracked down the Peruvian wheatgerm.

SIDNEY: Thank Holy Christ!

ESME: Thought you'd want to know ASAP.

ESME *leaves. Beat.*

LAYLA: Crisis averted.

SIDNEY: How long are you staying?

LAYLA: I'm here for a month all up. But I have other things to do. You're away most of next week, yeah?

SIDNEY: I'm afraid I couldn't cancel Berlin. First stop for the next album. But I'm not doing it forever, as I indicated during that first trip. I don't want to be Mick, you know, bouncing around sports stadiums as an octogenarian. There comes a time when one is bored by oneself, even if nobody else is.

LAYLA: No problem.

SIDNEY: I suppose you'll want to see some of the sights, too?

LAYLA: Actually, I know London quite well. I studied here.

SIDNEY: [*surprised*] Scholarship?

Beat.

LAYLA: My parents sent me to Cambridge.

SIDNEY: Oh. Wow… Wow… Come a long way, baby!

LAYLA: [*consciously*] Their alma mater. I did my MA there.

SIDNEY: Good for you.

LAYLA: Went home to work in the public service, against my parents' wishes. They wanted me to stay. Do law. Like them.

SIDNEY: [*slightly disconcerted*] Right. [*Struggling*] Gosh! Marvellous!

LAYLA: [*ignoring her*] So the next couple of days, I'll get a bit of a feel for the place. I'll come by tomorrow, then we'll resume when you get back.

SIDNEY: And we—?

LAYLA: We chat. It's not arduous. It's as much for you as it is for us. We want to know you're—

SIDNEY: I know—

LAYLA: Reality has landed—

SIDNEY: Sure—

LAYLA: We need to know—both parties—that it's the right thing, yeah?

SIDNEY: I know that.

LAYLA: To be sure. Let it sink in.

SIDNEY: So the home study—?

LAYLA: It's policy—
SIDNEY: Okay—
LAYLA: That we see you—
SIDNEY: Okay—
LAYLA: *Chez vous* as they say, in the domestic environment. That's from *our* end. At this end, you're good to go.
SIDNEY: It's a formality—
LAYLA: It's a formal step, yes.
SIDNEY: It's—
LAYLA: Part of the process. The IACT[1] has approved you, as you know. Now I have to make a recommendation to the committee—
SIDNEY: It's your recommendation that—
LAYLA: Yes—
SIDNEY: So you—
LAYLA: Well, put it this way: in four years, the committee has never voted *against* my recommendation.
SIDNEY: I see.
LAYLA: The final whatever—the go-ahead—
SIDNEY: Right—
LAYLA: We have to get through this to—
SIDNEY: Well, it's routine and routine—well, bureaucracy—
LAYLA: You said it.
SIDNEY: Sometimes there's no way around it.
LAYLA: Exactly. But there's no problem—I'm sure—
SIDNEY: Good!
LAYLA: It's as good as—
SIDNEY: Super Duper—
LAYLA: Dotting the 'i's'–
SIDNEY: Definitely.

Beat.

SIDNEY: It's just… I thought—
LAYLA: Sorry, you—?
SIDNEY: We had an understanding.

---

1 *Intercountry Adoption Casework Team*

LAYLA: An understanding?

SIDNEY: Yes, a—

LAYLA: An agreement?

SIDNEY: Not an agreement exactly, but a sympathetic—

LAYLA: We *are* sympathetic—

SIDNEY: And that things—

LAYLA: But there is now something of a sensitivity to how things are done, especially where—

SIDNEY: Where—?

LAYLA: *Celebrity*, is involved.

SIDNEY: Okay, alright—

LAYLA: Yes.

SIDNEY: Okay.

LAYLA: Yes.

SIDNEY: Alright.

LAYLA: Because with the spate of celebrity—

SIDNEY: Yes—

LAYLA: Attracting a certain degree of knee-jerk—

SIDNEY: Absolutely see that—

LAYLA: That's not going to be good for you, either.

SIDNEY: No. [*Beat.*] So technically—?

Beat.

LAYLA: The blue form.

SIDNEY: The blue form?

LAYLA: A signature.

SIDNEY: Okay. Good. A signature.

LAYLA: That's it. That's the whole—It's a signature and then she's—

SIDNEY: Okay. So that's—that's—*Whose* signature?

LAYLA: Mine.

Beat.

SIDNEY: I want you to know… it's not like… you know, a catalogue. It's not… When I picked her up, that first time, when I held her and… Something happened. [*Beat. Pulling herself back*] I've got a couple of meetings this afternoon but if you want to stick around—

LAYLA: Esme said she'll show me the house—

SIDNEY: I'll be through by four—

LAYLA: That's fine. [*Beat.*] We want to know this is the right thing for everybody, don't we?

SIDNEY: Yes.

LAYLA: And especially for Aamy.

SIDNEY: Yes. She's the most important one.

LAYLA: [*looking at the photo of the Queen again*] Hat, shoes and bag all the same colour, yeah?

SIDNEY: I believe so.

LAYLA: Very matchy-matchy.

SIDNEY: She kind of gets away with it.

SCENE FOUR

SIDNEY *and* ALFIE.

ALFIE: We're over.

SIDNEY: Over, Alfie?

ALFIE: Potentially over. If the album—

SIDNEY: You like the album—

ALFIE: Of course I fucking like the album—I'm your manager!

SIDNEY: But—

ALFIE: You know me, Sid, I do not paint the worst possible scenario unless every other scenario is firmly out of the picture.

SIDNEY: Which frankly—

ALFIE: It is. I've talked to Rick and Dick and Rodney but what they saw as a possibility is sinking over the horizon line.

SIDNEY: But Rodney said they believed—

ALFIE: I know what Rodney said—

SIDNEY: He and Dick said they saw enormous—

ALFIE: They never saw enormous potential, Sid. To be honest. They saw a chance and it was worth the gamble. But the record company thinks your clock is seriously ticking. Very Loud Ticks. [*Building*] TICK TOCK TICK TOCK TI—

SIDNEY: *All right!* That's not what they said when I signed.

ALFIE: They told you they loved you. They told you you've got something no-one else has.

SIDNEY: I'm a 'legend'.

ALFIE: You're a fucking legend.

SIDNEY: I *am* a fucking legend, Alfie.

ALFIE: You *are* a fucking legend, Sid. But *Supernova* was twenty-three years ago.

SIDNEY: What about Belarus? And Poland? Don't they count for anything?

ALFIE: I'm tremendously proud of your icon status in Minsk, love. But, weirdly, the record company is more interested in selling records in the US. As you know, that lot are ugly, ruthless, coke-snorting, bimbo-bonking bastards—

SIDNEY: That's why you identified with them, isn't it?

ALFIE: I'm with you all the way, babe. That's why I passed on Billie Gothic, even though she's sixteen and hot—

SIDNEY: She can't sing, Alfie—

ALFIE: Oh, stop *quibbling*, Sidney!

SIDNEY: Alfie, it's a medical condition. She actually has no vocal chords. Genetic disorder. Tragedy.

ALFIE: But she's hot. And sixteen. The singing is just the icing on the cake, these days.

SIDNEY: Oh, so what? I'm all icing and no cake? I'm just a big fat slab of icing?

ALFIE: I believe in you. I'm tied to you until I shuffle off this mortal coil, love. But the company will shaft you in the time it takes to air-kiss both cheeks, and I'm all you've got. It's close to over, Sid. If the album tanks, we're finished.

SIDNEY: Oh, Alfie, you really outdo me in the melodrama—

ALFIE: You're mortgaged to the hilt. You live like a rich person but you are not rich anymore.

SIDNEY: I'm rich-ish.

ALFIE: There's no 'ish' on the end of rich. It's like pregnancy. You are or you aren't. [*Beat.*] And you aren't. [*Beat.*] The bank has had enough. The HNI guy has been calling daily.

SIDNEY: Change banks!

ALFIE: We've exhausted the banks. The car people called. The insurance lot. Those dolts at the tax office sent a registered letter. And you're not taking this seriously, Sidney. The Shah of Iran or whatever's People are furious about your no-show—

SIDNEY: They wanted me to sing a Celine Dion song, Alfie!

ALFIE: It wouldn't have killed you.

SIDNEY: Yes. It. Would.

ALFIE: You stuffed the entire opening of the resort. They had to get Miss Congeniality Bahrain. Couldn't sing and a burqa would have done everyone a lot of favours, apparently. The Shah was furious.

SIDNEY: The Shah of Iran is dead, Alfie.

ALFIE: Prince Allah Akbar, whatever, who *contracted* you to do three nights at the Dubai Mirage—

SIDNEY: I had a sore throat, Alfie.

ALFIE: They're *arms dealers*, Sidney. If it's at all possible, one tries not to embarrass people who sell AK47s for a living. Your entire life is built out of polycarbons, like a film set, and pretty soon, the ill winds of the entertainment climate are going to blow it all over. Your star is no longer rising. It's descending. It's in the descendant. It's going *down, down, down*—

SIDNEY: I know what descending means!

ALFIE: We've reached the end of the road, babe. You're right on the precipice of… ironic.

A sharp intake of horrified breath from SIDNEY.

Beat. A very sober SIDNEY *takes this in. Now that she's listening,* ALFIE *starts playing her.*

However…

Beat.

SIDNEY: [*on tenterhooks, vulnerable*] Well?

Beat.

ALFIE: The Arbiter…

Beat.

SIDNEY: The Arbiter…?

ALFIE: He likes it.

SIDNEY: [*can't believe it*] *He likes it?*

ALFIE: He *loves* it—

SIDNEY: He used that word? He *loves*—

ALFIE: They never use that word, Sidney. It has never been articulated by a hack of any kind. But you could tell—

SIDNEY: You could tell—?

ALFIE: 'I want to go big on this' he said.

SIDNEY: He said that?

ALFIE: He said it. I heard it.

SIDNEY: Tell me again.

ALFIE: 'I want to go big on this' said he.

SIDNEY: The Arbiter.

ALFIE: The fucking Arbiter.

Beat, while they take in the immensity of what this means.

SIDNEY: So…?

ALFIE: It will be for the *front*—

SIDNEY: [*delirious*] The front!

ALFIE: The front of—

SIDNEY: The front of—?

ALFIE: [*quietly triumphant*] *The Sunday Magazine*—

SIDNEY: My God!

ALFIE: And they're flying—

SIDNEY: [*steeling herself for the wondrousness*] All right—

ALFIE: Jurgens Hurgens—

SIDNEY: Isn't that a yoghurt?

ALFIE: Does the Marc Jacobs campaign—

SIDNEY: Jurgens Hurgens!

ALFIE: Jurgens fucking Hurgens!

SIDNEY: Shooting me—

ALFIE: Upside down in aspic—

SIDNEY: Nice—

ALFIE: Naked on a camel.

SIDNEY: Uh-huh—

ALFIE: This is it—

SIDNEY: Alfie, I adore you. You know that, don't you? I adore you. And finally, *finally*—

ALFIE: Hold on, kitten. I want you to realise—

SIDNEY: Oh, I do, Alfie. I do, I do, Alfie!

Beat.

ALFIE: [*very serious*] You're going to have fire on all cylinders to let them know that this is a shiny new Sidney Jones who is absolutely, totally new-millennial. And that takes marketing. It takes strategy. It takes prostrating yourself before Beresford and being *everything he wants you to be*.

SIDNEY: I'm flat on my back, Alfie!

ALFIE: We need him to say *'You thought she was over, but baby, she's just beginning'*.

Beat.

SIDNEY: [*suddenly worried*] Jesus, Alfie… Maybe I *am* over.

ALFIE: That's not what I want to hear, Sidney.

SIDNEY: [*her anxiety building*] I don't know, Alfie. Sometimes I wonder if… I'm not hungry for it. The way I was.

ALFIE: Don't be ridiculous!

SIDNEY: [*occurring to her in the moment*] Apart from the money… and the profile… and the restaurant tables… and the free cosmetics, I'm not sure I see the thrill of it that much anymore.

ALFIE: [*tough*] Do you want to slide into ruin, Sidney? Is that what you want? Do you want to sing Oasis covers in pubs for the rest of your life, travelling around the provinces with some deadbeat alcoholic keyboard player in tight jeans and an eighties hairdo, amping up the sound levels because the punters would rather chat than listen to the old lady on the stage who does her own highlights because she can't afford a hairdresser? Is that what you want, Sidney? Going back every night to the Travelodge and getting into cheap sheets to read *Hello* coverage of Kylie dining at the Elysée Palace with Carla?

SIDNEY: [*snivelling*] No, Alfie, I don't.

Beat.

ALFIE: [*gentler*] Remember Edinburgh?

SIDNEY *smiles.*

SIDNEY: That was a long time ago, Alfie.

ALFIE: Back in the days when the term 'mother-fucker' only related to persons who had actually fucked your mother.

SIDNEY: Your father, basically.

ALFIE: [*wistfully*] Those were the days. The first tour. You were twenty years old and the sweetest little peach I'd ever laid eyes on.

SIDNEY: You corrupted me. Literally.

ALFIE: Someone had to. It was that little schoolgirl kilt you wore back then. White thighs and those sexy knee socks and I thought: *'This young woman is going to be the death of me'.*

They smile. Tender beat.

SIDNEY: I want the success, Alfie. But I also want the baby.

ALFIE: And you can have the baby, Sid. Just not yet. Not until the album's out and you're number one, again.

SIDNEY: I had a great time, Alfie. But I want this baby.

ALFIE: What you really *really* want is fame and fucking fortune, like you always have.

SCENE FIVE

JULIA *and* JOLYON, *Sidney's younger, handsome and rather louche boyfriend with an affected Cockney accent, are having a quiet beer in the sitting room. He is mid-anecdote.*

JOLYON: Balenci-fucking-aga. Right between Catherine Deneuve and Maggie Gyllenhaal and the chicks just keep coming. Lou Reed thumping, dazzling light spectacular, and girls with legs taller than me, I kid you not, and faces like angels, like angels that need cheering up, but you know, cheekbones wider than some European nations. Zero bazooks, but you can't have everything. And let me tell you, as someone who has rubbed knees with her, Catherine Deneuve is hot, grandma or no, so hot you'd need yoghurt to eat her, if you get my drift. Ouch! And let me tell you, she does not exercise, not a thing, zilch, sits around all day on her shapely arse being… Deneuve.

JULIA: Sidney could learn something—

JOLYON: Sidney could learn a lot—

JULIA: From Catherine—

JOLYON: French chicks—say no more—got the edge, don't they, always did—Brigitte herself before she turned into an animal nut, Beatrice Dalle, Isabelle Huppert, Carole Bouquet—A veritable shitload of Gallic beauty—

JULIA: I'm not sure that's the collective noun of choice—

JOLYON: You get my drift, Jules—sensuality is not enhanced by biceps—If fitness was the turn-on, I'd ask Becks for a date, wouldn't I? But who's going to tell her?

JULIA: Not me.

JOLYON: Not me.

Beat as they take this in, considering, mellow. JOLYON *cracks open another beer and passes it to* JULIA, *taking one himself.*

What's Midge up to tonight, then? Downloading KD Lang? Reading Jodie Foster's bio?

JULIA: At her mother's.

JOLYON: [*sighing*] What did she do wrong?

JULIA: *What?*

JOLYON: Midge's mother. Must be asking herself that question. Must trip off her tongue.

JULIA: You are incorrigible. You think that being witty disguises the fact that you're a serious homophobe.

JOLYON: You see, I just can't take that word seriously, Jules. It sounds like something a nerdy biologist uses to measure something. 'Can you pass me the homophobe? It's next to the Bunsen burner.'

Beat.

JULIA: So what do you think—?

JOLYON: Life? The universe? Beatles or the Stones? Straights versus bootleg?

JULIA: The baby.

JOLYON: The baby.

JULIA: The baby.

JOLYON: I defer.

JULIA: You defer?

JOLYON: If she's happy, I'm happy.

JULIA: That's a bit off, isn't it? I mean, you're the younger generation, you're supposed to—you know—*care*, have opinions—

JOLYON: I am?

JULIA: As a *young* person, it's *your job* to express strident ill-considered opinions! And here you are saying, if everything's hunky dory in my neck of the woods don't worry your pretty little head about gas emissions or poverty in the Third World or—or—

JOLYON: Christ.

JULIA: Well?

JOLYON: Fancy some dead meat?

She glares at him.

JULIA: [*realising*] Yes.

JOLYON: With the lot, extra bacon, medium rare?

JULIA: You order, I'll pick up.

JOLYON *speed-dials his mobile.*

JOLYON: [*into the phone*] Order for Burns, thanks. Two burgers please, medium rare, with the lot, extra bacon. And no special sauce… No. That's a 'no'. It's not very special, the special sauce, no offence. [*Hanging up*] Do you think the smell will evaporate before she gets home?

JULIA: We don't want a repeat of the KFC incident. She made my life hell for a week.

JOLYON: You see, that's my point. Nothing Catherine Deneuve loves more than a nice *filet mignon*, blue. And that's a turn-on in anyone's language. Every time Sidney orders a watercress salad the heat goes out of me. They could do tests: stick a bird in black latex in a restaurant with a naked man and see what the physiological consequences are of the woman's dining pleasure. Arugula: the shrivel factor. A nice sticky rib: bingo-bongo. There'd be a revolution in women's eating habits.

JULIA: You'd have to pay me a lot to sit next to a naked man while I was eating. It's remarkable that men have—the upper hand—with equipment that ugly.

JOLYON: You'd change your mind if you saw my 'upper hand', I assure you.

JULIA: I can see it now, Sidney comes home to find her PA eating meat while surveying her toy boy's member.

JOLYON: Need to chuck Midge in, Jules. Settle down with a Homo sapien instead of a homosexual.

JULIA: Midge *is* a Homo sapien, Jol.

JOLYON: Not from where I'm standing.

JULIA: What about the baby?

JOLYON: As I've said before, if she wants a baby, let her have a baby.

JULIA: It's not just a baby, Jol. It's a *black* baby.

JOLYON: Black, white, purple, a baby's a baby. I told her, I'll take it to the Wiggles 'cause I dig them—especially Murray—but I'm not changing nappies, not on your nelly, much as I love her.

JULIA: But it's going to have nannies and Start-rite shoes. It's going to hang out with other little Lord Fauntleroys, little Brooklyn and Cruz—

JOLYON: Nah, she's off Posh—

JULIA: You know what— [I mean]

JOLYON: Jeez Jules. Don't you think it's better to suffer from too much privilege than none at all?

JULIA: So you *do* have an opinion?

JOLYON: [*smiling*] Not just a pretty face, eh? And whatsit.

JULIA: It's amazing how often it comes up in conversation with you.

JOLYON: No, with *you*, Jules. It's the challenge, isn't it? I don't understand how you ladies do it, you know what I'm saying? What is it you *do* when you get intimate?

JULIA: You don't need to know.

JOLYON: [*faux naïve*] Maybe if I *watched*, I'd understand a little bit better.

JULIA: You're a wit, Jol.

JOLYON: That I am, Jules.

JULIA: *We'd* like to have a baby, actually.

JOLYON: Well, that's just wrong, Jules. Sorry. Draw the line somewhere.

JULIA: Because we're two women?

JOLYON: There's that. And then there's Midge's personality. We should be raising money to identify her gene pool and eradicate it forever, like malaria.

JULIA: You are a horrible person, Jol.

JOLYON: Getting yourself a turkey baster, then, Jules? Better get a big one. 'Cause I've heard size actually does matter. On the grapevine. That's the word. Size is all.

JULIA: I couldn't comment, Jol.

JOLYON: That's what I've heard, but don't quote me. Technique comes in at number two, right after sheer volume. Good news for me, of course, as they would be my first two characteristics in that department and in that order, not that anyone's interested. Size counts. My spies inform me, it's all about circumference. Just like a dining table.

JULIA: Is yours like a dining table, Jol?

JOLYON: Inasmuch as it is a large item around which attractive people congregate in order to have fun.

JULIA: Huh.

JOLYON: Don't get me wrong, Jules. I'm completely fine about the turkey baster bizzo—I'm only relieved that it won't be an actual turkey—but what interests me is that even for the straightforward purposes of manufacturing human beings, you and your sort couldn't just close your eyes and think of England. Or, I don't know, chocolate puddings. Women have been doing it for thousands of years. No-one I know personally, but as a general observation. Is it really that much more awful than sitting through a Michael Bublé concert? So who's the turkey?

JULIA: No idea, Jol.

JOLYON: Not necessary then? Dispensable info? Calling all sperm ponds? Jules, you've just never met the right bloke. [*Beat.*] A nice man. That's all I'm saying. But with a bit more of a feminine side than Midge.

JULIA: You sound like my grandma.

JOLYON: Oh, yuck! You mean your poor old granny is subjected to information on your unsavoury sexual preferences!

JULIA: Actually, Granny is quite *au fait* with diversity.

JOLYON: I do feel sorry for these old geezers who started out in a world with absolutely no diversity whatsoever and then find, at ninety-three, that diversity is the new homogeneity.

JULIA: Isn't that good?

JOLYON: All's I know is that you've obviously never been bonked by someone who knows his stuff.

JULIA: Like you.

JOLYON: I'm strictly a one-tyrant man. But for future reference…

JULIA: That's enough of that. She's probably got the place bugged. She's probably sitting in The Paranoia Room, some little antechamber up there— [*pointing to the ceiling*] —watching us on closed-circuit tele whilst eating a plate of Peruvian wheatgerm.

JOLYON: [*freaked*] Oohhhhh!

JULIA: Joking.

JOLYON: It's not about the *issues*, Jules. The baby's the thing. Only the privileged have a problem with privilege, Jules. I say that from experience.

JULIA: For God's sake, Jol, we all know your accent's put on.

JOLYON: Oi!

JULIA: You're a nice boy from Hove with a bank manager dad. All that stuff in *Rolling Stone* about your disadvantaged roots, jeez!

JOLYON: Got to have a profile, Jules. It's the way the world works. I've been pretending so long, it feels completely real.

SCENE SIX

SIDNEY *is strumming on her guitar, composing a song.* JOLYON *is reading a magazine.*

SIDNEY: I thought of a great line: 'He bows beneath her feminine mystique', but I can't think of anything that rhymes with mystique.

JOLYON: [*reading the paper*] Uh-huh…

SIDNEY: Unless… do you think 'Mustique' could rhyme with 'mystique'?

JOLYON: Not technically.

SIDNEY: If I went with Mustique and dropped mystique—

JOLYON: What? 'He bows beneath her feminine Mustique?' Sounds… sordid. What about her feminine *je ne sais quoi.*

SIDNEY: Oh, thanks so much, Jolyon.

JOLYON: What about 'her feminine ways'? Then you've got 'haze', 'daze', you've got 'days' as in weeks, you've got 'stays', 'craze', you've got 'crays' as in crayfish—

SIDNEY: Reassuring—

JOLYON: —and 'maze'. 'He bows beneath her feminine ways and then… gets lost in Hampton Maze.'

SIDNEY: I don't know about Hampton Maze. It's a pop song not a picnic guide.

JOLYON: Listen, love, some of the greatest lyrics in history are completely incomprehensible. What about Shakira: 'My breasts are small and humble, so you don't confuse them with mountains'.

SIDNEY: Remind me to tell Esme that while we're in Berlin, Dwayne's dropping in some swatches.

JOLYON: What's wrong with the Rolex?

SIDNEY: Bits of fabric.

JOLYON: [*still reading the paper, not fully concentrating*] Oh, got you. Strange moniker for an interior decorator, don't you think? Dwayne Hiscock?

SIDNEY: It's pronounced 'Hiccough'.

JOLYON: Does that make it less strange?

SIDNEY: We're contemplating a *trompe l'œil.*

JOLYON: Never really got those. I mean, it's not as if you walk into a dining room in Chiswick and go: 'Oh look, there's Lake Como in the distance', eh? You go: 'Oh, look, there's a picture of a lake on the dining room wall'. And then you might go: 'Wankers'.

SIDNEY: I haven't eaten anything except broad beans for three days. I wanted to look svelte for Berlin. Do I look thinner?

JOLYON: No.

SIDNEY: I'd have to be thinner, wouldn't I? Only eating broad beans?

JOLYON: Depends how many broad beans you ate. Shouldn't you be gobbling string beans?

SIDNEY: How do I look, Jol? Young?

JOLYON: Childlike.

SIDNEY: Seriously. For a thirty-six-year-old.

JOLYON: You look old for a thirty-six-year-old. But for a woman of your age, you look excellent.

SIDNEY: I'm not much older than thirty-six, be fair. A couple of years.

JOLYON: *Dog* years.

SIDNEY: I want a baby, Jol.

JOLYON: [*putting down the paper*] I know, dearest.

SIDNEY: You know, something happened, Jol. When she looked at me. I know you think it's all voodoo rubbish, but I swear, she looked at me and I looked at her and *something happened to both of us*.

Beat. JOLYON *looks at her carefully.*

What if she doesn't sign the form?

JOLYON: [*tenderly*] Babe, it's not the end of the world.

SIDNEY: I held her, Jol.

JOLYON: I know you did, Sid.

SIDNEY: I touched her. I smelt her. She looked at me.

SCENE SEVEN

ALFIE, JULIA *and* JOLYON.

ALFIE: He's our man.

JOLYON: He's our man?

ALFIE: Possibly the most influential journalist in the entire city thinks the album is a goer when every other hack wants to throw her in the has-been pit with Pat Benatar.

JULIA: So what you're saying is—

ALFIE: He has to love her. He has to believe in her. And he has to tell the world.

JOLYON: Frankly, I think you're worrying too much, Alfie. I don't see that it's a problem.

ALFIE: No, I'm sure you don't, Jol. And I'll tell you why, shall I?

JOLYON: Tell me why, Alfie.

ALFIE: Because you're a fucking idiot.

JULIA: He's just a little bit slow, Alfie. It's natural after the drugs.

JOLYON: Those days are long gone, Julia.

ALFIE: After that many, you're probably better off sticking with them, Jolyon. You could make a fortune going around schools as a one-man anti-drug program. Kids would just look at you and run screaming towards wholesome pursuits.

JOLYON: Honestly, Alfie, there's one word missing from your vocabulary: *trust*.

ALFIE: Oh, I do trust you, Jolyon. I trust you to stuff everything up.

JOLYON: I understand the business.

ALFIE: Not to put too much of a point on it, but I see you primarily as a piece of sexual apparatus. You're there to service her needs. I'm there to keep her in the loop. You're not in the loop, business-wise. Speaking business, you're loop free, you're a loop-free zone.

JOLYON: Okay, the loop is not my thing. But I have common sense, Alfie.

ALFIE: That's why you set fire to the curtains in the Hyatt Regency in Minneapolis.

JOLYON: That was my younger, screwed-up, delusional, self. I've done therapy since then.

ALFIE: Aromatherapy. Half the time I talk to you I honestly think there's nothing at all in there—

JOLYON: [*proudly*] I'm just internally online, Alfie. I'm physically present but I'm metaphysically surfing.

ALFIE: Internally online!

JOLYON: You don't think much of me, do you, Alfie?

ALFIE: Not at all, Jol.

JOLYON: [*confused*] What does that mean?

JULIA: Be nice, Alfie.

JOLYON: You're just angry because you know you could have managed me. I gave you the option and you blew it.

ALFIE: As I said, ad nauseum, I'm a one rehabilitation at a time man.

JOLYON: I've still got a lot to offer the world of rock-and-roll. If you had vision, you'd see that.

ALFIE: [*ignoring him*] Impending motherhood is only going to confuse the issue. I don't want either one of them sidetracked while this profile is in the pipeline. *Comprendez*?

JOLYON: No word about the baby.

ALFIE: I'm trying to bring out the Amy Winehouse in her and subdue the Mia Farrow, all right? So don't mention Africa.

JOLYON: That could be tricky.

JULIA: *How*, Jol?

JOLYON: Comes up, doesn't it? *Out of Africa. African Queen*. I'm going to have to be on red alert.

ALFIE: Have you heard of Miyamoto Musashi, Jolyon?

JOLYON: Isn't he the sushi chef at Nobu?

ALFIE: He was a martial arts master of the sixteenth century. One of history's greatest swordsmen. He said, 'You win battles by knowing the enemy's timing and using a timing which the enemy does not expect'.

JOLYON: Wow.

ALFIE: Artists thrive on spontaneity and instinct but those who care for artists must protect them with *brutal strategy*. We must defeat the nay-sayers and the cynics who seek to bring them down. It's my job to read the currents of the zeitgeist, to take the temperature of the philosophical trends, to lip-read the global whisperings. That's *my* job. And that is how I know that *this is the man who can establish Sidney's comeback bona fides in a major fucking way and nothing can go wrong*. People listen to Beresford. He can draw a line under who she was and give the thumbs up to who she is now—

JOLYON: It's hard to do the thumbs up if you're drawing a line, Alfie.

ALFIE: The record industry is in a state of imminent collapse. *Downloading*. Do you know what that means, Jolyon?

JOLYON: You stick a disc in and you press—

ALFIE: *Death*. That's what it means, Jolyon. Death. Doom. Bankruptcy. This record may be the last chance Sidney has to make any real money. If this album doesn't crack it, her entire destiny is *Celebrity Get Me Off This Island.*

JOLYON: The album will be huge, Alfie. Have a bit of faith, man!

Beat as ALFIE *and* JULIA *stare glumly.*

A bit of marketing. A few glowing write-ups. A couple of jabs of Botox.

ALFIE: Sidney has not had a record on the charts since 1996. Billie Gothic and her ilk were in *kindergarten* in 1996.

JOLYON: *But who wants to listen to them, Alfie*?

ALFIE: Well, *I do*, Jolyon. Because youth is golden, my friend. It's the only non-commodity left in the human experience and there is not a person alive who is not in love with it. Five years and then it's over. Goodbye serious money. Hello cabaret circuit. Up there in the spotlight, varicose veins, smeared mascara singing 'The Rose'.

JULIA: You or her?

ALFIE: Tobias Beresford does not need to be distracted by a tiny, homeless African.

SCENE EIGHT

The sitting room of SIDNEY*'s house.* JOLYON *is sitting with* TOBIAS BERESFORD. *They have a couple of beers in front of them.* JOLYON *is very relaxed in his own domain.* TOBIAS *looks a bit less at ease—but he's not under-confident. They're both conscious of filling in time until* SIDNEY *arrives.*

JOLYON: Get you down, does it? The horror with which your chosen profession is routinely greeted by the general population.

TOBIAS: I don't take it personally.

JOLYON: Why not?

TOBIAS: Because I don't write for… a muck-raking publication, do I?

JOLYON: I wouldn't care to hazard a guess.

TOBIAS: The press is the cornerstone of a thriving democracy.

JOLYON: Oh, absolutely. You're right there. Of course, once you've seen Britney Spears without any knickers on, you do start wondering about the benefits of a totalitarian regime.

TOBIAS: *The Times* doesn't print photographs of a knickerless Britney.

JOLYON: *Yet*. Anyway, aren't you all going down the gurgler? Print media's over, isn't it?

TOBIAS: Not quite.

JOLYON: World wide web versus parochial, perishable paper. Everyone's jumping ship, Tobias.

TOBIAS: I'm clinging to the railings, Jolyon. Extraordinary talent is my life vest. That and the TV show.

JOLYON: Papers can't compete in the end. Little box on your kitchen bench. Endless repertoire of information. At your fingertips. Absolutely free. It's frugal to google.

TOBIAS: But ink helps you think.

JOLYON: It's all about following the link, Tobias. You're like a butter salesman in the early eighties. Or a postman in 1876 when Graham Alexander Bell first yelled down a wire at his assistant: 'Watson, come here; I want you'. The world is marching on, mate.

TOBIAS: Bit of a media analyst, are you?

JOLYON: Armchair variety. You bet your sweet bippy.

TOBIAS: Sidney has a bit of a love-hate thing with us, doesn't she?

JOLYON: Oh, Sidney has a love-hate thing with everything. Not to be sexist or anything, but women, *hard work*. You can see why men shack up and watch Judy Garland movies just to avoid the Feminine Mood Swing. Almost. You're not—are you?

TOBIAS: I'm comfortable with who I am, Jolyon.

JOLYON: [*slightly askance*] Not that I've got an issue—

TOBIAS: That would be awful.

JOLYON: Love them. Elton. Ricky… Noel—Coward—*Mister* Coward to you and me—

TOBIAS: I'm sure they're immensely relieved.

JOLYON: It's just I never feel absolutely relaxed in the company of our effeminate cousins. You know what I'm saying? I'm always worried they're dissing my sartorial style.

TOBIAS: While we're waiting for her, I wonder if you'd mind if I asked you a couple of questions. Just personal interest.

JOLYON: Fire away. I'm delighted you have any personal interest in me, so few do.

TOBIAS: What was the real reason you left the band? I mean, your last album sold two hundred thousand records. You won the Brit for best new band. And then in Minneapolis, inexplicably, you just walked out, two hours before a sold-out gig.

JOLYON: And never came back.

TOBIAS: And never came back.

JOLYON: The hotel curtains.

TOBIAS: I beg your pardon?

JOLYON: Didn't like 'em. I was sitting in the hotel and I realised that I just didn't like the curtains.

TOBIAS: The curtains didn't please you?

JOLYON: Sounds trivial, I know. But you probably don't get the full picture. They were flecky. Sort of orangey puce. Not really seventies—not ironic. Just ugly. And I thought, 'I'm going to be facing a lot of ugly curtains in this life and I'm not sure I can really handle that'.

TOBIAS: Why didn't you tell *Rolling Stone* that?

JOLYON: I didn't think they'd really appreciate it. If it had been *House and Garden*, I would have. Besides which, I'm trying hard to create an enigma. That way my descent into obscurity will seem intriguingly reclusive rather than just pathetic.

JOLYON: But what about Sid, then? Cracker album.

TOBIAS: It's good.

JOLYON: It's *seriously* good.

TOBIAS: It *is* seriously good.

JOLYON: Going to do it justice, I'm hoping.

TOBIAS: The album will be a whole section of my piece, obviously. The themes running through it, the hint of coming through a period of beating up on herself to being more accepting, the return to lyricism, punctuated by some very real, very tough, very urban, and may I say, very authentic rock-and-roll.

JOLYON: I like that. How's it feel to be 'The Arbiter'—?

TOBIAS: That's silly, that name. Not my idea.

JOLYON: People listen to you. That must be fun, holding people's reputations in the palm of your hand—

TOBIAS: I try to be responsible—

JOLYON: You say someone's the real deal and people buy records. S'pose you get propositioned a lot.

TOBIAS: Young, talentless blondes coming out of my ears.

JOLYON: With blondes, talent just confuses the issue, don't you find?

TOBIAS: You could be a very useful part of this profile, Jolyon.

JOLYON: Oh no, mate. No, no, no. I've been told to keep *stum*.

TOBIAS: Is Alfie behind that?

JOLYON: It's all about controlling the image, mate.

TOBIAS: I want to write a complex piece, Jolyon.

JOLYON: [*pleased with his wit*] And I'm sure you will. You're complex. She's complex. And I have a complex. A curtain complex.

TOBIAS: Greatest feelgood song of all time?

JOLYON: Without a shadow of doubt: [*beat*] 'Everything I do'.

TOBIAS: [*disbelieving*] *Bryan Adams*? You're playing with my mind, aren't you?

JOLYON *sings 'Everything I Do', beginning with 'I would fight for you' and singing to the end of the song, finishing with the title line. Beat.*

JOLYON: [*pondering the beauty*] Fuck me.

Awkward beat.

TOBIAS: Where is she, by the way? Julia said—

JOLYON: I'll check. Meanwhile I'll send in some coffee—

TOBIAS: I'd appreciate it—

JOLYON: Forgive us if we're all slightly wary of the press. Great Divide, isn't it? Those who do and those who comment.

TOBIAS: Where do you fit, Jolyon?

JOLYON: Oh, I'm neutral. In every department: talent, opinion. Zero ideological content but nothing not to like, know what I'm saying? Human Switzerland.

JOLYON *exits.* TOBIAS *speaks into his tape recorder to check it's working.*

TOBIAS: Testing, one, two, three. [*Singing badly*] *'Be my, be my, be my little baby... wah-ah... be my—'*

He doesn't notice that the door opens. LAYLA *sticks her head in. She stops and watches/listens, amused by his awful singing as he plays it back. Suddenly he notices her, takes her in for a second and breaks off.*

Oh, Earl Grey if you've got it, thanks. Drop of milk. No sugar.

LAYLA: No sugar?

TOBIAS: And I could do with a snack.

LAYLA: A snack?

TOBIAS: If that's okay.

LAYLA: Anything else, sir?

TOBIAS: No, that would be perfect.

LAYLA: Toasted sandwich?

TOBIAS: Lovely.

LAYLA: Ham, cheese, tomato? What's your fancy?

TOBIAS: Ah… any of the above.

LAYLA: Salt? Pepper? Mustard? Pickles?

He looks at her quizzically. She steps into the room.

Dancing girls?

TOBIAS: I'm sorry?

LAYLA: Care for dancing girls with that?

TOBIAS: [*quietly aghast*] You're not the maid, are you? [*Beat.*] Oh shit. [*Beat.*] I'm a journalist.

LAYLA: Congratulations.

Beat.

TOBIAS: Look, sorry—

LAYLA: It's okay. You *assumed*—

TOBIAS: I—

LAYLA: You made an assumption—

TOBIAS: Listen, I'm—

LAYLA: A racially-based assumption—

TOBIAS: I'm *black*—

LAYLA: Oh! Oh, *thank you*. Thanks for telling me. You're off the hook then. Because black people never make racially-based assumptions.

TOBIAS: Jesus, you're hard work! [*Studying her*] Are you a friend?

LAYLA: I'm visiting.

TOBIAS: From…

LAYLA: Pluto.

TOBIAS: Lovely. Just over for the weekend, then?

LAYLA: Theatre. Galleries.

TOBIAS: Not a lot of theatre on Pluto?

LAYLA: There is, but it's light-years from what's happening here.

TOBIAS: [*realising*] *I know you.*

LAYLA: What?

Beat.

TOBIAS: [*placing her*] Cambridge, '01.

She studies him.

LAYLA: Shit.

TOBIAS: You're—

LAYLA: Oh—

TOBIAS: You—

LAYLA: Yes—

TOBIAS: Layla.

LAYLA: [*trying to remember*] Yes—

TOBIAS: Tobias. Small world.

LAYLA: You were friends with that guy—Harvey, that weirdo—

TOBIAS: You're the one who—

LAYLA: Yes. I was the sucker talked into a blind date—

TOBIAS: He's dead now.

LAYLA: Oh, good.

TOBIAS: Oh yes… Coming back to me… You were famously haughty.

LAYLA: Is that so?

TOBIAS: Your mum was a judge back in…?

LAYLA: Good memory.

TOBIAS: Your dad ran some headhunting operation—

LAYLA: *Recruitment*. Headhunting could have the wrong connotation coming from a racist like you.

Beat.

TOBIAS: You went back?

LAYLA: Job came up.

TOBIAS: Anna told me. Remember—

LAYLA: Yes.

TOBIAS: Told me.

LAYLA: That's right.

TOBIAS: Said you were in public policy… You always had that look about you. Like you weren't going to waste time.

LAYLA: Like you.

TOBIAS: Like me.

LAYLA: What happened to your band? You were going to take the world by storm, I recall.

TOBIAS: We took the world by light breeze.

She smiles. Beat.

LAYLA: Don't let me interrupt your little performance.

TOBIAS: [*attempting to cover embarrassment*] Greatest feelgood song of all time. The Ronettes.

LAYLA: Good. But not as good as 'Close to You'.

TOBIAS: I can't feel good about the song thinking of Karen Carpenter wasting away. The Ronettes *ate*.

LAYLA: 'Close to You'. The greatest.

TOBIAS: But she sang it with her *brother*. Doesn't that strike you as unsavoury—?

LAYLA: You're strange.

TOBIAS: Greatest feelgood of all time. You can judge a person on the basis of that one question.

LAYLA: Did I pass?

TOBIAS: I'm reserving judgement. To see if there are mitigating factors. What the hell are you doing here?

LAYLA: Strangely, they allow me in every so often.

TOBIAS: No, I mean, *here?*

LAYLA: Bit of work stuff. Nothing interesting.

TOBIAS: [*puzzled*] You're—?

LAYLA: [*quickly*] Legal—

TOBIAS: You did law after—?

LAYLA: Thought it might come in handy—

TOBIAS: So—?

LAYLA: [*faultless*] Represent a concert operator in Jo'burg. Putting together a bit of a music festival thing—

TOBIAS: What? With *Sidney?*

LAYLA: Sort of a middle-aged 'In the Park'. More your HRT crowd than your GBH crowd—

TOBIAS: Interesting—

LAYLA: Vineyards—

TOBIAS: Vineyards?

LAYLA: Concerts in vineyards in the wine region around Jo'burg—

TOBIAS: Never knew there was a wine region around Jo'burg—

LAYLA: Punters come to see old rockers and drink wine. Some serious money there for people like the guy I'm working for—

TOBIAS: Who is—?

LAYLA: [*dredging creatively*] Reggie. Winter— [*tiniest beat*] Bottom.

TOBIAS: [*buying it*] Like your job?

LAYLA: Good money. Nice boss. Not forever.

TOBIAS: Very good. Very economical. Do you do speed-dating?

LAYLA: It usually takes me more than three minutes to find true love. You?

TOBIAS: I have an occasional stutter which more or less counts me out. Takes me three minutes just to say 'Gemini'.

LAYLA: You're not stuttering now.

TOBIAS: Beauty relaxes me.

LAYLA: You're good.

TOBIAS: Actually, I'm very, very bad.

LAYLA: *Actually*, it's coming back to me. You always were a smooth-talker.

TOBIAS: I have a trick.

LAYLA: Is that so? What's your trick?

TOBIAS: I believe everything I say.

LAYLA: That makes you different?

TOBIAS: Compellingly so. Don't you remember?

LAYLA: No.

TOBIAS: That's because you were too busy shagging that dolt in the Drama Club.

LAYLA: Sebastian, the now very rich gynaecologist.

TOBIAS: Oh, you gave him a hand with his early training.

LAYLA: He didn't need *another* hand. Believe me.

TOBIAS: Otherwise he was a pompous, deluded, hairy, smug, reactionary prick.

LAYLA: Some things you're prepared to overlook.

He laughs.

TOBIAS: How could you not have considered me?

Beat.

LAYLA: I considered you.

TOBIAS: [*chuffed*] You did?

LAYLA: Nanosecond.

TOBIAS: But?

LAYLA: I thought: Give him a decade. He'll improve.

TOBIAS: Your Masters in soothsaying, then?

LAYLA: So you *have* improved?

TOBIAS: Beyond your wildest dreams.

She laughs.

LAYLA: Married?

TOBIAS: *Oh my God, no.*

LAYLA: Kinky?

TOBIAS: Only in a good way.

LAYLA: Know any good pubs?

TOBIAS: Thought you'd never ask.

SCENE NINE

SIDNEY *and* JULIA. SIDNEY *is dressing for the interview and very nervous.*

JULIA: He's been waiting for an hour.

SIDNEY: [*het up*] I'm attempting to get ready. I'm attempting against all hope to elicit some support, some assistance from one of the many staff I employ at vast expense!

JULIA: I think you're ready, Sidney.

SIDNEY: It's a creative sounding-board I'm after. It's more than a *dresser*, Julia.

JULIA: [*calmly*] I'm sorry, Sidney. Shall we go down, then?

SIDNEY: Honestly, do I have to do everything myself? I'm living my life so alone!

JULIA: There are people who are dedicated to your needs, Sidney.

SIDNEY: Oh, you're all looking after your own little interests!

JULIA: What about Nikki?

SIDNEY: Publicists don't count! They're just *around* like *pollen*.

JULIA: There's marketing.

SIDNEY: Marketing! Pffff!

JULIA: There's your agent. Your business manager, the lawyers.

SIDNEY: Idiots!

JULIA: There's your stylist. Hair and make-up. Facialist. There's your psychoanalyst, the Indian yogi—

SIDNEY: Oh, Yogi-Schmogi!

JULIA: The nutritionist, personal trainer, of course. Not forgetting the neurolinguist to change negative thought patterns—

SIDNEY: What a triumph, she's been!

JULIA: There's your psychic—

SIDNEY: She's fired. Which she didn't see coming, by the way. *Ergo* she's fired.

JULIA: Naturopath. Kinesiologist. Osteopath. Chiropodist. There's Soong-Chee-Twat—

SIDNEY: Soong Chee What?!

JULIA: The Korean nail woman.

SIDNEY: *Ridiculous* name!

JULIA: It's *her* name, Sidney. [*Going on*] And then there's Esme. And there's me.

SIDNEY: Oh, not forgetting Miss Important!

JULIA: Well, no.

SIDNEY: You're not hearing me, Julia! *I'm suffocating in support persons.*

JULIA: Well, you can't do without me, Sidney.

SIDNEY: Sometimes I think your ego is *quite* out of control!

JULIA: So who can you do without? Shall we start with the Soong-Chee-Twat?

SIDNEY: *Don't be ridiculous.* Why are you holding me up? It's *your* fault he's been waiting for an hour!

JULIA: Of course it is.

SCENE TEN

TOBIAS *is alone in the sitting room, with remnants of tea and cake.* ESME *sticks her head in.*

ESME: She's nervous.
TOBIAS: She doesn't need to be nervous.
ESME: Julia apologises. Says she's moments away.
TOBIAS: I appreciate the tea. Good brew.
ESME: No trouble.
TOBIAS: That was the best fudge slice I've ever had. What's your secret?
ESME: [*pleased*] Real butter.
TOBIAS: What *is* real butter?
ESME: I keep a secret stash. But don't tell Her Highness.
TOBIAS: Tucked away behind the yak protein supplements?
ESME: My baking skills are wasted here. I won prizes for my Yo-Yos.
TOBIAS: We'd all die happy if we could make that claim.

ESME *laughs.*

If I become very rich and famous will you come and work for me?
ESME: I'll think about it.
JOLYON: What's the greatest feelgood song of all time, Esme?
ESME: 'Dancehall' by Bunny Wailer.

He's shocked by her knowledge.

TOBIAS: Seriously great fucking choice. If I was only a few years older, Esme, I'd be on your case.
ESME: Now you're really buttering me up.
TOBIAS: You tick most of my boxes. Quick. Sexy. Good cook. It's just that, boringly, I go for the under-seventies.

She smiles.

How long have you worked for her?
ESME: Started out doing her hair for TV appearances, when she was twenty years old, and then when things went mad a few years later, she got me to run the household. We know each other's secrets.

TOBIAS: Of course, she was awfully young when *Supernova* came out, wasn't she? Not many nineteen-year-olds could write those lyrics—

ESME: She's wasn't nineteen! She was twenty-four!

TOBIAS: [*triumphantly*] I knew it!

ESME: [*realising*] *Oh dear*.

TOBIAS: Obviously she slept with whoever did her Wikipedia. [*Attempting to seduce*] Come on, Esme, talk to me, darling!

ESME: You're a very sneaky young man. I'm not telling you any of her secrets.

TOBIAS: Give us a hint, Esme.

ESME: [*playing*] Make it worth my while?

TOBIAS: What's your poison? Cold hard cash?

ESME: A wildly erotic interlude.

TOBIAS: [*very amused*] You're a naughty, naughty girl, Esme. Did anyone ever tell you that?

ESME: Plenty. But not since 1967.

TOBIAS: I'd bet you were a bit of a looker.

ESME: [*trying not to be pleased*] That was not an uncommonly held view. Keith Richards said I was the wildest ride he ever had.

TOBIAS: Ooh, you little trollop! Serious?

ESME: Serious.

TOBIAS: Full of surprises. Come on, darling, you could really round out this piece.

ESME: You bet I could. But I'm not going to.

SCENE ELEVEN

TOBIAS *and* SIDNEY *in the sitting room. They shake hands.*

TOBIAS: Thanks for… capitulating.

SIDNEY: No problem.

TOBIAS: I'm faintly starstruck.

SIDNEY: Oh, it's mutual, Mr Beresford.

TOBIAS: Come on!

SIDNEY: You seem to be everywhere: newsprint, on the tele—

TOBIAS: I'm riding a bit of a media wave, but you're—well—
SIDNEY: Careful—
TOBIAS: Iconic.
SIDNEY: Uh-huh.
TOBIAS: The stuff you must have seen over the years. Mixed with some pretty extraordinary characters—Veritable line-up of rock royalty—
SIDNEY: That's true.
TOBIAS: Dated Joe Strummer, didn't you?
SIDNEY: Yes. Before he died, obviously.
TOBIAS: John Entwistle.
SIDNEY: Old Thunderfingers.
TOBIAS: Dead, though.
SIDNEY: What a way to go.
TOBIAS: Bit of a flingette with Shaun Ryder—
SIDNEY: Virtually dead.
TOBIAS: Whatshisname from the—
SIDNEY: A while ago, now.
TOBIAS: Shame about the Alzheimer's.
SIDNEY: *Any*way—
TOBIAS: It's a genuine pleasure.
SIDNEY: Normally Nikki, my publicist—
TOBIAS: I know. But I really, really hate it when publicists sit in.
SIDNEY: It must be awful for you having them there. Reminding the subject that you are, essentially, on a search-and-destroy mission.
TOBIAS: Oh, I don't mind that at all. I just find it annoying when they hit on me after the subject's left the room.
SIDNEY: Funny.
TOBIAS: You look great, by the way.
SIDNEY: Thank you.
TOBIAS: Bit of a gym bunny?
SIDNEY: I'd rather lie around on a *chaise longue* eating chocolates but that's a punishable crime these days.
TOBIAS: Ready for the launch, then—?
SIDNEY: I am actually. I think it's sounding—

TOBIAS: Classy.

SIDNEY: Alfie tells me—you—

TOBIAS: Yes—

SIDNEY: You—

TOBIAS: I liked it.

SIDNEY: [*camouflaging her gratitude*] Well—

TOBIAS: I genuinely liked it.

SIDNEY: Okay, so—

TOBIAS: *A lot.*

Beat.

SIDNEY: [*staying calm*] So I'm not going to be pilloried—?

TOBIAS: I don't pillory. I can't even spell it.

SIDNEY: Can you spell 'patronise'?

TOBIAS: Okay, guilty as charged. On occasion. But I wouldn't patronise you, Sidney. As Dame Edna said, 'You're an icon with mike-on'.

SIDNEY: Okay, then, so—

TOBIAS: I think I get you.

SIDNEY: [*interested*] What makes you think that?

TOBIAS: Brutal truth?

SIDNEY: Absolutely.

TOBIAS: You were a very talented young singer who struck gold just a fraction too young. You made an album that managed to briefly unite the vacuous pop crowd and the iconoclastic punks because it was edgy and optimistic and original. Then you faded from view doing the circuit, playing songs you should only ever do for encores. Now you've made an album that might possibly be the perfect evolution of your first album. There's something true about it and slightly unnerving and very… hopeful. It's got some catchy tunes but it doesn't feel cynical. You may very well be onto something.

SIDNEY: Okay, so—?

TOBIAS: I'm not interested in cliché.

SIDNEY: Frankly, I thought that's all you lot peddled.

TOBIAS: Actually, I thought it's all *you* lot peddled.

SIDNEY: I beg your pardon?

TOBIAS: You want me to pay you the respect you deserve, then *frankly*, I think you should deserve it. You use us. We use you. It's a mutually profitable relationship. The dislike is just a subterfuge for the general public. They *like* you more if you pretend to hate us. They *read* us more if we pretend to hate you. But I'm not going to—

SIDNEY: You're not?

TOBIAS: The point is—

SIDNEY: The point is—

TOBIAS: It's a fabulous album.

SIDNEY: Sorry, I'm deaf.

TOBIAS: The album is fabulous.

She smiles. He smiles.

I'd like to have you on the show: bit of a preview, sing a little ditty as a getting-to-know-you for a new audience. Then follow up with a major piece more specifically on the album in the *Sunday Magazine*.

SIDNEY: [*containing herself*] Sounds… fine.

TOBIAS: I've been doodling away with my intro whilst waiting, actually. [*Flicking through his notebook*] 'Ever since Phoenix hit the ancient gossip circuit by rising from the ashes, popular culture has thrilled to the notion of spectacular comebacks. There's nothing that the public love more than the notion of redemption, the idea that someone lost is refound, someone dismissed is rekindled, someone dead is revived. Tarantino reinvented Travolta, the BBC ignited Jane Austen and Britney Spears came back from madness and worse, pudginess, to hit number one again. But no revival is likely to top that of Sidney Jones…'

Beat.

SIDNEY: Don't edit that, will you?

He smiles. Beat.

TOBIAS: I want you to show me the real you.

SIDNEY: What if I'm not her yet?

TOBIAS: Then this can be the annunciation.

SCENE TWELVE

Blackness. The roar of a stadium crowd. The theatrical lights come up. SIDNEY *is in front of a microphone on a stage, facing the crowd.*

SIDNEY: [*in basic German*] Hello Berlin!

Roar of the crowd in response.

Jemand erzählte mir sie Kerle wissen, wie man sich gut unterhält! [Somebody told me you guys know how to have a good time!]

Roar of the crowd as music starts.

Wollen sie lust heute Abend haben? [Do you want to have fun tonight?]

Roar of the crowd.

SCENE THIRTEEN

Post coital. The bed. Tobias' flat.

LAYLA: I didn't realise when you said you'd 'show me the sights' that this is what you had in mind.

He flashes her.

TOBIAS: 'Big Ben'… Oh, you meant the *other* one.

They smile.

I should have got my doctor's approval before doing that. You're dangerous.

LAYLA: Sissy.

TOBIAS: If we'd gotten around to it at Cambridge, the future of the world would have been different.

LAYLA: I wasn't that good then.

TOBIAS: Is that so?

LAYLA: I've been honing my skills. What's for dinner?

TOBIAS: Needy, aren't you? Require servicing on all fronts. [*Beat.*] When are you going home?

LAYLA: Friday week.

TOBIAS: I think I want you to stay.

LAYLA: You *think*, you do?

TOBIAS: If I didn't qualify it, I'd look, you know, overly keen.

LAYLA: So you do?

TOBIAS: It was that line about honing your skills. I've always had a hard spot for cavalier women.

LAYLA: No-one's ever called me cavalier before.

TOBIAS: A cavalier woman is all *any* man fantasises about.

LAYLA: I have to finish this job.

TOBIAS: Finish it and come back.

LAYLA: Need to weigh my many and varied options.

TOBIAS: Cool customer.

LAYLA: You're a journalist, Tobias. As we all know, you would and almost certainly have put your mother on eBay for a good story.

TOBIAS: Off duty.

LAYLA: No such thing.

TOBIAS: Well, if you won't surrender, will you at least agree to a diplomatic détente?

She smiles.

[*With a touch of lasciviousness*] With bells on?

They kiss. Withdraw. Beat.

What would your parents think about you coming back?

LAYLA: It wouldn't cross my mind to consult them.

TOBIAS: Not on good terms?

LAYLA: I don't talk to my father. I'm not going to bore you with this—

TOBIAS: I won't be bored.

LAYLA: Had an affair with their maid. How tacky is that?

TOBIAS: Actually, I've always rather fancied the whole maid idea. As you know.

They kiss.

[*Casually*] Who else is doing the vineyard thing—?

LAYLA: Who else?

TOBIAS: On the ticket. Curious. Who's big down there—?

LAYLA: Oh, lots of golden oldies. You know…

TOBIAS: Yeah?

LAYLA: [*extemporising, not quite as good as she was*] Simon and Garfunkel might do it. Bit of luck.

TOBIAS: Yeah? Who else?

LAYLA: Annie Lennox is in. Which is… super. Robert Palmer—endless phone calls—He's a maybe.

TOBIAS: He's a maybe, is he?

LAYLA: Bit of a nightmare. Hard to handle.

TOBIAS: Oh, well he would be, wouldn't he? Given he's dead.

LAYLA: He's not dead!

TOBIAS: He's dead.

LAYLA: That was fast! I was only talking to him on Tuesday.

Beat. She realises she's busted.

TOBIAS: I don't even think you've got a law degree. I don't think you'd know a legal tort from a sacher torte. [*Beat. Thinking aloud*] Okay, so. [*Beat.*] It's top secret… Africa… International travel… You're a spook.

LAYLA: There you go again.

TOBIAS: MI5? No. Let's be logical about this. [*Musing*] I bump into you in some rock-and-roller's palazzo… Cambridge… you did social policy… international relations… You're… here because… hold on… because… [*Beat.*] Shit. [*Beat.*] *She's buying a fucking baby.*

LAYLA: I cannot comment on—

TOBIAS: Holy shit!

LAYLA: Neither confirm nor deny. You don't know that—

TOBIAS: My God!

LAYLA: Look—

TOBIAS: All fits. The album: *Reaching Out*—

LAYLA: Listen, I—

TOBIAS: Can I ask you a couple of questions?

LAYLA: No, you cannot.

TOBIAS: I'm going to get the lowdown somewhere.

LAYLA: I can't comment—
TOBIAS: Okay. *I'm right!*
LAYLA: Jesus! I can't talk about people's private—I have an obligation to *protect*—
TOBIAS: Okay!
LAYLA: I'm *serious*.
TOBIAS: I can see that!
LAYLA: I could get in serious trouble.
TOBIAS: *All right.*
LAYLA: *I cannot say anything at all.*
TOBIAS: I get that—But I'm just wanting to chat—
LAYLA: I can't compromise—
TOBIAS: I *know*. [*Beat.*] Old times' sake.
LAYLA: I didn't like you, *then*.
TOBIAS: And on the basis of that, I've spent ten years remodelling myself. You owe me.

She smiles, despite herself.

Just, you know, flutter your left eyelash if it's a yes. [*Beat.*] That was a flutter! You fluttered!
LAYLA: *I blinked.* [*Beat. She smiles.*] Can I trust you?
TOBIAS: Look at this face.
LAYLA: That's why I'm asking.

SCENE FOURTEEN

Berlin. JOLYON *and* JULIA. *The sitting room of luxurious hotel suite.* JULIA *lies listlessly on the sofa drinking beer while* JOLYON, *beer in hand, surveys the DVD library. Lots of empty beer bottles, both tipsy.*

JULIA: Why didn't you want to go out with her?
JOLYON: With a bunch of sweaty Deutsche record execs?! *Nein Danke.* They'll go somewhere Joel Grey is emceeing. Some basement beer-hall full of old Krauts. I told her it's separate suites tonight. I need my beauty sleep.

JULIA: Shall we ask room service to bring us something completely mad and then go out of our minds when they can't do it?

JOLYON: Vegan *coq au vin*.

JULIA: Salmon tartare. Medium.

JOLYON: [*finding a DVD*] Okay, allllll rigggggght. What do we have here? *Voilà!*

JULIA: No!

JOLYON: I haven't said anything yet.

JULIA: No. No. No. Not again.

JOLYON: You don't know what I was going—

JULIA: I do. *Das* fucking *Boot*.

JOLYON: Oh, Jules, they've got it!

JULIA: I will not watch it again, Jol. No way, Jose.

JOLYON: [*whingeing like a kid*] Oh, Juuuuuullllllleeeees.

JULIA: I watched it at the Ritz in Paris, I watched it in Moscow. I watched it in Rome and I'm not watching *Das Boot* again.

JOLYON: But we're in Berlin, Jules. Where we should have watched it first.

JULIA: I'm not watching *Das Boot* in Berlin, Jol. It will send me into a state of paranoid delusions. I'll be walking down the *Friedrichstrasse* trying to calculate how old the pedestrians would have been in 1943.

JOLYON: They're all scattered beneath the thriving suburban lawns of Buenos Aires, Jules. [*Sulking, still combing the list*] What do you want, then?

JULIA: I don't care what it is as long as it's nothing at all to do with babies.

JOLYON: Okay—

JULIA: You know my rules: no defence forces, no prison, no junkies. And no babies.

JOLYON: *Baby Magic*. Lindsay Lohan and Ben Affleck star in this rollicking—

JULIA: No Ben Affleck. And nothing 'rollicking'.

JOLYON: *Hello Dicky Bird*, starring Myra von Travis and Elsinore Sludge—

JULIA: There's a movie called *Hello Dicky Bird*?

JOLYON: I made it up.

JULIA: I was getting quite excited.

JOLYON: *Baby Labs.*

JULIA: Did I or did I not say 'No baby movies'?

JOLYON: But this sounds rivetting, Jules: 'When Gwen Struthers (Natalie Portman), a luckless in love dog walker meets Tom Baker (Josh Hartnett), a hapless dog impounder about to lose his job unless he succeeds in capturing one more stray, the doggy do really hits the fan and unleashes a barkingly funny comedy—'

JULIA: No. Isn't there *any* Denzel we haven't seen?

JOLYON: You see that's where your lesbianism just doesn't ring true, Jules. When it comes to films, you're as straight as they come. [*Flicking through the choices*] *Bringing Up Baby*?

JULIA: You are kidding me, aren't you, Jol?

JOLYON: [*flicking*] *Baby Boom? Rosemary's Baby? What Ever Happened to Baby Jane? Million Dollar Baby?* Oh, here we go… *Juno?*

JULIA: No! My God!

JOLYON: Looks like it's *Das Boot*, love.

JULIA: Why do you like that film so much, Jolyon? Open up to me so that I may comprehend.

Beat.

JOLYON: [*slowly, with growing passion*] Well… first of all, it's the way the U-boat descends beneath the surface of the sea. The way it tilts and then riffles through the waves and then disappears and you know that this fine group of young men, who through no fault of their own are Krauts, are entering a strange new world of tension and madness and fear and claustrophobia and tinned sauerkraut. I find that moving, Jules. And when the curmudgeonly but honourable captain makes them go deeper and deeper… [*voice of the German captain*] *'150 metres…160 metres… 170 metres… 180 metres'*, and the U-boat is creaking and the bolts start to pop off the steel walls, and we all know in seconds the sub is going to be crushed by the weight of the water and they're doomed, they're doomed, it's over and then finally, sweat dripping, he says, [*captain's voice*] *'Take her up'*, and we know how close they've come to annihilation in the inky fathoms, Jules. And then the scene, where the young war correspondent has the flannel covered in oil flung in his face and he looks at them all, humiliated, as the officer says quietly, 'Who did that?' And then barks, 'WHO DID THAT?!', because even though the war correspondent is an intellectual who wouldn't know a spanner from a… a… and the other sailors look down on him for it, he's doing an important job in telling the world the truth about the horrors of war. And then after they torpedo the English convoy and they're standing in the funnel thing watching the destroyer break up and the sky is all glowing with the aftermath of battle and they see the English sailors jumping from the bridge into the flaming oily water screaming in pain and there etched in their faces is the recognition that there but for the grace of God go them. And what about the moment when the war correspondent says he's… [*tearing up*] … leaving the sub and gets the, the, the young guy with the—with the pregnant [*choking up*] French girlfriend to give him the letters he's written her for him to deliver and… there are [*tearfully*] *hundreds* and you know and he knows and we all know that *he's never going to see her again* because it's war, Jules. It's *war*. It's terrible, awful war and they're Krauts and we fucking won, didn't we?

Beat. She puts her arm around him, sweetly.

JULIA: [*softly*] I s'pose you better put it on, Jol.

JOLYON: [*immediately recovered*] I love you, Julia. You know that, don't you? And this will be the definition of perfection: lying nude, between the crispy starched German sheets of a posh hotel, drinking a lovely bottle of plonk courtesy of our own personal commandant, watching a bunch of men in uniform running around a submarine.

JULIA: Jolyon. Put it on.

JOLYON: Do you think when I yell 'Up periscope' you'll put all hands on deck, Jules?

SCENE FIFTEEN

Continuation of Scene Thirteen. TOBIAS *and* LAYLA *in the bedroom of his flat.*

TOBIAS: You're not going to, are you?

LAYLA: Why not?

TOBIAS: *Why not?*

Beat.

LAYLA: I like her.

TOBIAS: She's a rich, self-obsessed celebrity who's used to getting exactly what she wants.

LAYLA: I like her, *underneath.*

TOBIAS: You don't even know her.

LAYLA: I don't know you, either.

TOBIAS: What's that supposed to mean?

LAYLA: It's my job to make swift assessments. To have a feeling.

TOBIAS: You give babies away on the basis of your *feeling?*

LAYLA: Well… yes.

TOBIAS: You'd have to be very confident about your 'feelings'.

LAYLA: I am.

TOBIAS: So do you think women like Sidney are doing the right thing?

LAYLA: Can't talk about Sidney. You know that, you shameless, agenda-laden exploiter of opportunities.

TOBIAS: Women *like.*

LAYLA: It's not my—

TOBIAS: But it is. It's quite literally your 'business'. I'm interested in how you feel about the work that you do.

LAYLA: I have a job, yeah?

TOBIAS: That's a start. Tell me about it.

LAYLA: I work in a bureaucracy that is well-intentioned but not always efficient. I make assessments on the basis of my instinct and intelligence. I have an objective but interested eye. What about *your* job?

TOBIAS: I work in a bureaucracy that is well-intentioned but not always efficient. I make assessments on the basis of my instinct and intelligence. I have an objective but interested eye.

Beat. They smile.

LAYLA: Okay. You tell me. What do we do?

TOBIAS: What do we do?

LAYLA: What do we do with little black babies?

TOBIAS: I think we should keep out of the way, actually. If we're not going to do any good we should just get the fuck out of there.

LAYLA: Let them look after themselves, hey? Stand on their own two feet. Take a little responsibility.

TOBIAS: I believe in help. I don't believe in *PR exercises*. I don't believe in getting what we want out of Africa and making out that it's all about what *we* can do *for* a continent we really don't give a fuck about.

LAYLA: You don't give a fuck about Africa?

TOBIAS: *I* do give a fuck, actually. As you have had *amply* demonstrated… You need to get educated.

LAYLA: A Masters from Cambridge no good to you, then?

TOBIAS: About the real world. A *trillion* dollars has gone to Africa in the last sixty years. Has a trillion dollars stopped genocide, misery, AIDS, corruption? Western compassion has *killed* African entrepreneurship: *You're dirty, you're hopeless, you're sick.* Western aid has filled the coffers of the dictators because it keeps on coming whether those evil fuckers listen to their people or not. All this, and they want to take the babies, too.

LAYLA: *Cynic.*

TOBIAS: *Realist.* Sidney's desire for that baby is just self-interest masquerading as love and that is the core of Western benevolence. Western governments *want* the aid agencies to handle Africa—'You tell us what the policy should be. We're in your capable hands.' This they say to a bunch of twenty-somethings on the ground in Somalia or Rwanda or Ethiopia who wouldn't know a workable strategy from an iPod manual. *They're kids.* They want to spend a bit of time showing how morally integrated they are and then, after a few years, they'll head back to Connecticut and look fondly back at their character-building years in the war zone.

LAYLA: Am I trying to show how morally integrated I am?

Beat. He calms down.

TOBIAS: [*lightly*] No, it's been made perfectly clear that you have no morals at all.

LAYLA: What about Darfur? What about Ethiopia? What? The West should just get back to Pilates?

TOBIAS: What's aid done? It's brilliantly achieved the institutionalisation of corruption. Sidney and her performance at Band-Aid. What a fucking joke, that was. Geldof—nice guy, dead ugly, no rocket scientist.

LAYLA: People gave vast amounts to Africa after that.

TOBIAS: And virtually all of it went to propping up the Ethiopian government whose army had caused the famine in the first place so they could feed their militias and force the kids coming for food to enlist. And all the time the government was getting pats on the back by the West for its humanitarian conscience. And the good people of Holland Park or Dorset or Wyoming were reassured that they were nice, caring people even though they go skiing.

LAYLA: But that's your fucking fault! You, the media. Isn't that a great little story?

TOBIAS: Yes, it's my fault. And it's Rupert's fault. And it's the fault of all those wilfully blind bleeding heart ninnies out there who buy the papers and want to believe in the magnanimity of their fellow rich white humankind.

Long beat. They look at each other intently.

LAYLA: Are you a good journalist?

TOBIAS: No.

LAYLA: Why not?

TOBIAS: I care too much.

LAYLA: Isn't that good?

TOBIAS: No.

LAYLA: Why not?
TOBIAS: Because the bosses don't want heart.
LAYLA: Why don't they?
TOBIAS: The heart is ungrammatical.
LAYLA: I've never heard a journalist talk about 'the heart' before.
TOBIAS: I'm a bad journalist, but I'm a genuine original.
LAYLA: Are you trying to make me fall in love with you?
TOBIAS: I'm a fatalist. If I have to try, it won't work.

She looks at him. She's falling.

SCENE SIXTEEN

Post-show. A Berlin bar/club. SIDNEY *is sitting in a roped-off booth.* KURT, *a handsome, sleazy German man in a slightly dishevelled very expensive suit, slides in next to her with drinks.*

KURT: I think we maybe saw each other in Gottenburg?
SIDNEY: At that place—
KURT: *Ja*. All those crazy people.
SIDNEY: You're Berlin-based, though, no?
KURT: *Ja*. I'm here now. I was in the New York office for eighteen months but the Yanks drive me nuts.
SIDNEY: Why is that?
KURT: They take themselves so seriously.
SIDNEY: Uh-huh.
KURT: Their superiority complex really gets me down. You know while they were running around throwing tea in the Boston harbour like a bunch of crazy people, Mozart was writing his string quartets in Vienna eating sacher torte.

SIDNEY *laughs flirtatiously while failing to understand.*

I really loved the show. I think the album's going to blow the hosen off everyone.
SIDNEY: I'm seriously hoping to blow the hosen.
KURT: You look incredible.

SIDNEY: Really?
KURT: You work out, *ja?*
SIDNEY: *Ja*. Seriously.
KURT: It shows, *ja?*

He starts casually fingering the button on her blouse.

SIDNEY: [*aware, but not alarmed*] *Ja. Ja.* I hope so.
KURT: I like this blouse. Blouse? *Ja?* Or 'shirt'?
SIDNEY: Blouse is absolutely correct.
KURT: I like animal prints.
SIDNEY: Me too.
KURT: They make you wonder, *ja?*
SIDNEY: That's the idea.
KURT: If there's a tiger inside.
SIDNEY: Or an ocelot.
KURT: Is there a tiger, Sidney?
SIDNEY: What do you think, Karl?
KURT: Kurt.
SIDNEY: Kurt.
KURT: I think I'd like to find—

KURT *pops the button, which flies off into the shadows.*

SIDNEY: Oh fuck.
KURT: I'll find it.
SIDNEY: We're going to need a goat.

SCENE SEVENTEEN

TOBIAS *and* LAYLA.

TOBIAS: Friday.
LAYLA: Friday. That's the deadline.
TOBIAS: Coming back?
LAYLA: Play your cards right.
TOBIAS: Marry me.
LAYLA: Almost certainly not.

TOBIAS: Like many who have gone before me, I'm going to pin my hopes on 'almost'.

LAYLA: You hardly know me.

TOBIAS: I have a feeling and I know you're big on feelings.

LAYLA: I'll wait and see if I miss you.

TOBIAS: Finally! The modern definition of love.

LAYLA: I'm reserving judgement.

TOBIAS: Your specialty, isn't it? I'm in love with you.

LAYLA: That was quick.

TOBIAS: You work fast.

LAYLA: You fall fast.

TOBIAS: If it wasn't fast, it wouldn't be falling.

LAYLA: True.

TOBIAS: Fast. Deep. Furious. But perfectly judged and very occasional.

LAYLA: Are you serious?

TOBIAS: This is where I say: 'I've never been more serious in my life,' but I have been. Or I could say: 'I've never felt like this before', because I haven't. Okay. So let's go with that. I've never felt like this before. You're much too smart for me but I'm hoping you want a man who preserves your sense of superiority. You're beautiful. You make my fingers tingle when you walk in a room. I want to stockpile every glimpse of you. You've single-handedly devastated my ongoing sense of personal misfortune.

She laughs.

Tell me you're in love with me.

LAYLA: I can't do that. I want to keep you hungry.

TOBIAS: I swear I'll stay hungry.

LAYLA: That's what they all say.

TOBIAS: You are, though, aren't you?

LAYLA: You worry me.

TOBIAS: That's not my fault.

LAYLA: Do you know how to be happy?

TOBIAS: Not yet. But if you won't be my wife, you could be my tutor.

SCENE EIGHTEEN

Television studio. TOBIAS *is interviewing* SIDNEY. ALFIE *watches from the wings. Through the course of the interview, the sense of a studio audience diminishes as the focus intensifies solely on* TOBIAS *and* SIDNEY.

TOBIAS: [*to the audience*] She first came to public attention with her early eighties album *Supernova*, a young woman's feisty proclamation to the world that she was going to do things her own way. It was a prelude of what was to come. For almost three decades, Sidney Jones has rolled with the punches of a fickle industry to produce a number of albums that have run the gamut from quirky to querulous, louche to lacklustre, and garnered her five top ten hits, including the somehow unforgettable (and take that as you will) 'What Am I Called'. Her upcoming album is *Reaching Out* and it's a whole new Sidney Jones from the perky upstart of the past. The new album promises to be a powerful and classy *cri de cœur* from a woman who started out a bit too spangly for street cred. She's boogied her way from Minsk to Manchester and bonked her way across many rock-and-roll beds. Here to tell us more about it is the still very sexy lady herself: Sidney Jones.

Recorded applause.

SIDNEY: [*pleased*] I don't know whether to be flattered or furious!

Recorded laughter.

TOBIAS: We're about to be deluged by the rantings of the fourth estate as the album hits the streets but I want to leave all that spin behind and talk about the real Sidney Jones.

SIDNEY: Is this the part where I lie down on the couch, Dr Freud?

Recorded laughter.

TOBIAS: I'm sure it wouldn't be the first couch you've reclined on, Sidney.

Recorded laughter.

It's been a long career but it seems as if in many ways it's been a lonely one—

SIDNEY: Oh, it's lonely at the top, Tobias.

Recorded laughter.

TOBIAS: It's brief at the top, as well, isn't it?

More laughter.

SIDNEY: Sweetie pie, I was at the top when you were just a glint in your daddy's eye.

More laughter.

TOBIAS: Touché. But let's get down to the nitty-gritty, Sidney. Your latest heart-throb is Jolyon Toss, aka The Tosser.

SIDNEY: Neither of us like that nickname very much.

TOBIAS: He's a nice feller, actually. But he's just the latest in a long line of riff-raff rock and rollers. You're not in the first blush and yet, no hubby. Is a public life all-consuming?

SIDNEY: Oh, Tobias, a girl has to have variety.

Laughter.

TOBIAS: No baby, either. Any regrets on that score?

SIDNEY: As the Little Sparrow said, *je ne regrette rien*. What doesn't kill you makes you stronger.

TOBIAS: Is that true, Sidney?

SIDNEY: Is it true?

TOBIAS: Well, you're adopting a baby. Surely that's some kind of acknowledgement of sacrifices made along the way?

She laughs.

SIDNEY: [*a moment of disbelief*] What?

Beat.

TOBIAS: Word has it. Care to give us the lowdown, Sydney?

SIDNEY: I—*I want a child.*

TOBIAS: What lead you to the moment of realisation? [*Looking at the studio audience*] We want to know, don't we, people?

Recorded hollers and claps. Beat. She rises to it.

SIDNEY: It's a—It's a collection of emotions that become—

TOBIAS: Go on.

SIDNEY: Yes, all right. It's a hunger.

TOBIAS: At what point does having a baby become—a fixation?

SIDNEY: At the point when it seems to be slipping away from you.

TOBIAS: What makes some women feel that hunger? What is it about them?

She thinks.

SIDNEY: They know that to feel love they have to… give it.

TOBIAS: You're chasing love?

SIDNEY: Who isn't?

TOBIAS: So do you think they're better-looking?

SIDNEY: *What?*

Beat.

TOBIAS: African babies.

Beat. SIDNEY *is shell-shocked.* ALFIE, *in the wings, looks stricken.*

Because it's not an English baby you've chosen, is it? It's not actually a local baby. It's not from, say, Leeds. There must be a few single mothers in Leeds that are adopting out, no? A couple of sixteen-year-old locals, eh, who had a quick unthinking shag? It's not from Liverpool or Cornwall or Wales, is it? You're shopping around for an African bub?

SIDNEY: I—I—

TOBIAS: Little black cutie pie? Big eyes? Looking out at you saying *Take me! Take me!*

SIDNEY: Adoption waits for English babies are much, much longer. It can be years and I can't wait years.

TOBIAS: But you *did* wait years. Forgot to have one, didn't you?

SIDNEY: I had a career. I'm not the only woman who's made that mistake.

TOBIAS: [*neutral*] All the rage, now, isn't it? Everywhere you look there's a glamour puss fed-exing a stork over to the Third World. Let us all in on the musings, Sidney. Where does this baby hunger come from?

Beat.

SIDNEY: Is it explainable?

TOBIAS: Well… babies crisscrossing the globe… little African orphans winging their way towards nannies… It ought to be explainable, don't you think?

SIDNEY: [*gathering strength*] If in finding a child I can also play some small part in alleviating an intolerable reality, why not?

Smattering of applause from the audience.

TOBIAS: That's lovely. Selfless.

SIDNEY: Most selflessness is the combination of desire and opportunism, isn't it?

TOBIAS: What about your life? Is that a life that is really going to be good for a child?

SIDNEY: What?

TOBIAS: Come on, Sidney. The travel, the long hours, the company you keep. It has to be considered—

SIDNEY: Do you say that to the female barristers? To the surgeons? Women are busy these days. It's virtually a pre-requisite for *being* female.

TOBIAS: Most female barristers aren't strutting around stages in fishnets—

SIDNEY: You're going to punish me because I make my living with a guitar?

TOBIAS: Plonk an orphan in a rock-and-roll life and cross your fingers?

SIDNEY: Most nights I'm at home watching 'Masterchef' and drinking carrot juice. The only law I've broken in several decades is the law of good taste. And that's basically because no-one wants to see a rock singer on stage in a wimple.

Laughter from the audience.

TOBIAS: Does it bother you that some people would argue you're removing a child from their own culture?

SIDNEY: Do you think the kids in African orphanages for years and years are engaging with their cultural heritage?

TOBIAS: And what would you say to people who say you're playing a part in an entrepreneurial scandal that's continuing to wear down the morale of the Third World and disenfranchise children from their birthplace?

SIDNEY: I'd say that love is more important than territory, that a child is more important than an ideology, that the truth is more important than a story.

TOBIAS: You're quite smart, aren't you?

SIDNEY: [*tough*] Am I smarter than Angelina?

TOBIAS: What's this about, Sidney?

SIDNEY: I think it's about you crossing a line.

TOBIAS: [*utterly certain*] And I think you're throwing a massive temper tantrum about your creaky biological inadequacies.

SIDNEY: Who could blame me?

TOBIAS: Well, I could. [*Beat.*] You've realised that money can't buy you love itself. But it can buy you a little piece of Africa. A borrowed child. A facsimile of love.

> SIDNEY *stares at him. A long moment as they lock eyes, surreally suspended from the reality of where they are. Blackout.*

SCENE NINETEEN

JULIA *reading* The Times. *The headline reads: 'Sidney Puts Aamy on Amex'. An utterly ruined* ALFIE *listens, alongside* JOLYON, *googling on an Apple laptop, as* ESME *surveys another copy of* The Times.

JULIA: [*reading*] 'The question remains what price is paid and by whom when Sidney Jones wants to be a mother? Some might say that the Arbiter went too far in his late-night interview on his eponymous show, but the fact is it's hard to feel sympathy for baby hunger when you know it comes hard on the heel of money hunger, fame hunger and Botox hunger. One of our most revered compatriots once wrote that money can't buy you love, but in Sidney Jones' case, it can buy you an orphan'.

Beat.

ALFIE: [*desolate*] Goodbye Grammies. Goodbye features on how Sidney Jones is embedded in the pop musical psyche of a nation. Hello women's magazines on how she's decorating the nursery and a fucking media frenzy. Goodbye big fucking yacht. Goodbye dreams. Farewell. Farewell… Over the horizon line… Bye-bye… Bye-bye dreams! Off they go with the little ducks that never came back.

JOLYON: [*googling*] No-one's even mentioned the album.

ALFIE: There was a mention.

ESME: Something about a 'triumph of optimism over experience' in the *Independent*, wasn't there?

JOLYON: [*googling*] *Guardian* has a special feature: 'Are African Adoptions Saving the Children or Saving our Celebrities?' *Independent* has: 'The Angelina Agenda: Rescue Mission or Fashion Accessory?' The *Daily Mail*'s headline: 'Sidney Seeks Sambo'.

JULIA: Oh, nice.

SCENE TWENTY

TOBIAS *and* LAYLA. *Both impassioned:*

LAYLA: You had no right to do that!

TOBIAS: Like you, I'm paid for my opinion.

LAYLA: You hijacked her and you used me!

TOBIAS: She was there with her eyes wide fucking open. She knows how the media works!

LAYLA: She didn't stand a chance. It was totally unfair. And using pillow talk to facilitate your dirty work is very fucking tasteless!

TOBIAS: I don't play fair when I'm right.

LAYLA: And you're always right.

TOBIAS: Most of the time. If I didn't think that, I couldn't do my job. I'm not going to play fair with her in the same way that I wouldn't play fair with a genius young singer who happened to be a neo-Nazi or paedophile.

LAYLA: I don't give a shit about you and your rationalisations. I care about the child. No-one is interested in this child except Sidney!

TOBIAS: *I'm* interested in the child. But there's only one thing that creates an actual emotion, that *inspires* an emotion in a wealthy white woman, there's only one trigger than launches any feeling at all for the Third World, and that's a baby. And sorry, but that makes me angry.

LAYLA: So what? While the world gets its act together to defeat global misery, we just stand back and *wait?*

TOBIAS: It's not working, Layla. Babies are being stolen, their parents are being coerced because they've got no choice.

LAYLA: This baby is not stolen. She's not kidnapped. Her parents have not been coerced.

TOBIAS: I don't think saving a child, one by one, is going to change anything.

LAYLA: [*shocked*] *What?*

TOBIAS: There's a systemic problem, Layla.

LAYLA: My God, Tobias. She's a systemic problem *with a beating heart.*

TOBIAS: It's *human trafficking*. Like virtually all Western interference, it's making the fucking problem bigger.

LAYLA: Her name's Aamy.

TOBIAS: [*unmistakably personal and growing in intensity*] I don't want *Aamy* co-opted for a multi-billion-dollar industry. I don't want some tiny baby in some struggling fucking orphanage in some dusty fucking town on the edge of nowhere—I don't actually want that child to be lifted up into strange white arms and carried onto a jumbo fucking jet to be transported away from everything it's smelt and everything it's felt and every sound it's heard and everyone it's known and *the whole fucking fantastic catastrophic marvel that is Africa.*

Beat.

LAYLA: [*stunned*] How old were you?

Beat.

TOBIAS: Eighteen months.

LAYLA *sits down.*

LAYLA: Where from?

TOBIAS: Kibera. A shanty town outside Nairobi.

Beat as she absorbs this.

LAYLA: Have you been back?

TOBIAS: [*dispassionately, repressing the feeling*] Two years ago. The woman who ran the orphanage actually remembered me. Nice lady. Said I used to stand on the sides of the cot like I was looking for someone.

LAYLA: She remembered that?

TOBIAS: She probably thought: 'I'd better give him a memory because he's got none'. No fucking memories.

LAYLA: How long were you there?

TOBIAS: Few days. No reunions. Everyone dead, gone, dispersed. Just a hole. Shitty little place. Stinks. A town. I was nothing to it. It was nothing to me. I might as well have been writing a Lonely Planet guide. Walk two streets north and you'll find a decent burger.

LAYLA: What happened to your birth parents?

TOBIAS: Father unknown. Mother died in childbirth.

LAYLA: Who adopted you?

TOBIAS: Nice, kind, educated, middle-class people.

LAYLA: You poor thing.

TOBIAS: I know.

Beat.

LAYLA: Where would you be?

TOBIAS: Where would I—?

LAYLA: If we left the babies in Africa?

TOBIAS: Not in a Bloomsbury bedsit with a beautiful woman.

LAYLA: 'Babe'.

TOBIAS: Babe.

LAYLA: So it's not just knee-jerk left-wing intellectual fashionability that makes you such a troublemaker?

TOBIAS: Well… that too.

Beat as she takes it in.

My parents had an attitude that it didn't matter what colour you were, you were human. They patted themselves on the back so that when it came to me and my pale-skinned, fair-haired brothers, there was no difference between us. I lived in a white family in a white town in a white world. And every time I looked in the mirror I expected to see a white face. Every time I looked in the mirror, I thought, 'Who the fuck is that?' I was white. I *felt* white. And then I'd go out into the world and people would yell, 'Hey, darkie! Blackie! Jungle bunny!' 'What? *Me*? *I'm not black*, you racist cunt!' I'd see docos on Africa and it might as well have been Mars. These snotty savages running around in the dust… what the fuck were *they* to *me?* And this is what I've learned, Layla. That if you look in the mirror and you don't see yourself, you're in big fucking trouble.

LAYLA, *exhausted by their equal passions, walks over to him. She touches his hand.*

We are what we have come from. Not something *borrowed*. Not something *acquired*. It's the taste and smell and touch of the earth you were born into. Every single child you pluck out of Africa and drop in a white Western lap is living an artificial life and eventually, *they will feel it.*

LAYLA: Are you sure about that?

TOBIAS: I'd give my life to prove that. [*Beat.*] I already have.

SCENE TWENTY-ONE

SIDNEY *and* LAYLA *at the house. Mid-conversation. Urgent tempo.*

LAYLA: The family, the family environment, the familiar—these are the best options.

SIDNEY: But that's not always possible—

LAYLA: I'd be the first to agree. But it's the most desirable permanent solution. After that, relatives or close adults, so their environment stays familiar, yeah?

SIDNEY: If that's an option.

LAYLA: That's the permanent life plan which works best for the child. No argument with that. But as you say—not always possible.

SIDNEY: Remember, the life she'll—

LAYLA: The life you—

SIDNEY: Well, yes. Yes, I mean. I want to give her everything. She'll—

LAYLA: What? Come a long way, baby. [*Beat.*] Article Twenty Paragraph Three of the CRC provides that 'when considering solutions, due regard shall be paid to the desirability of continuity in a child's upbringing and to the child's ethnic, religious, cultural and linguistic background'. We have to look at the personal characteristics of the child's individual situation to determine the most appropriate protective measures.

SIDNEY: Yes, of course, but—

LAYLA: Each child is unique—

SIDNEY: Of course, but—

LAYLA: We have to consider the circumstances of the life in question—family history, age, health, mental and physical, family, friends, character, religion, ethnicity—

SIDNEY: Character? She's fourteen months old.

LAYLA: My sense is that when they emerge, they are not just receptacles for inculcation. They have—*we* have—character—

SIDNEY: Okay, but—

LAYLA: The UN Convention on the Rights of the Child and the Hague Convention both establish that family reintegration is what we're really after—'The child, for the full and harmonious development of his or her personality, should grow up in a family environment'.

SIDNEY: But this baby doesn't have—

LAYLA: Technically—

SIDNEY: She's all alone—

LAYLA: Not quite all alone. She has—

SIDNEY: She has—no-one—

LAYLA: She has Africa.

Beat. SIDNEY *studies her. Growing horror.*

I have to be sure.

Beat.

SIDNEY: What's going on?

LAYLA: I'm… I'm not…

Beat.

SIDNEY: What's wrong with me?

LAYLA: Not *everything's* about *you*. It's a life. It's a human life we're trafficking in, aren't we? However we like to put it.

Beat.

SIDNEY: What?

Beat. Silence.

You're going to listen *to him?* One journalist wants to beat up a story and—

LAYLA: That's not why he—

SIDNEY: Of course it is! It's all about ratings—

LAYLA: He cares about this—

SIDNEY: It's completely cynical—

LAYLA: It's *real* to him—It's *means* something—

SIDNEY: What?! [*Beat.*] *You're defending him?*

LAYLA: *It's not about him.*

Beat. SIDNEY *is catching up.*

SIDNEY: It was— [*Beat.*] Oh, right. [*Beat.*] Got it. [*Beat.*] You told him. It was you.

Silence.

LAYLA: I never wanted that to happen.

SIDNEY: You've listened to *him*, Layla. Now, listen to *me*. I'm going to honour that little girl. I'm going to pay my dues to who and what she's come from. I am not going to obliterate her history. I'm not going to deprive her of her story, the story so far. I'm giving her *another* story. She can have two stories. Can't she? [*Beat.*] Can't she?

SCENE TWENTY-TWO

JULIA, ESME, ALFIE *and* JOLYON *are sitting around the sitting room.* SIDNEY *is sitting slightly apart.* JULIA *reads from* The Times.

JULIA: [*reading*] 'Of course one person's accessible is another person's derivative and where one sits on this will most likely inform whether this is really the comeback Jones was quite literally banking on. For my money, despite some positives, the new album never quite hits the mark and reminds those of us submerged in the industry that a good album has to feel like an evolution not a game plan. A comeback, after all, is God-given not man-made.'

Silence.

ALFIE: [*finally, wearily*] What is it about me? What is my problem? Why do others roll in clover while I'm lying thirsty in the dust? Do I not work hard enough? Do I not bleed? Do I not love and nurture my people? Have I not earned a dose of karmic peace and wealth? [*Beat.*] At my age I should be lying back on a yacht while Billie Gothic commissions keep me in Rothkos.

JULIA: Roth*kos* or Roth*mans?*

ALFIE: I'm not a philistine, Julia. I know my Cy Twomblys from… the other one. I'm a signed-up member of the Tate Modern, got contemporary art oozing through my pores, Jules.

JULIA: [*knowing*] What was the last show you saw there, Alfie?

ALFIE: [*trying*] Big things with stuff all over them—paint and—painty splodges, stuff and whatsit all over. Colour. Paint. Whatever. [*Beat.*] Okay, well. It's over. Moving on. [*Reading the paper, trying to dismiss*] Oh fuck me, the Red Herrings are at number one. Sometimes you really have to wonder at the intelligence of the general population. No fucking A and R man with any kind of brain matter would sign up those brain-dead, pimply-faced plagiarists if they were the last rock-and-roll band on earth and yet, and yet, *someone did.* Some complete coke-addled, musically-illiterate lunatic on a major fucking expense account had their big-breasted very do-able assistant, Amber or Dusty or Beccy, slip the CD in the deck and went: 'Okay, all right, this little piece of complete wankery is going to suck in the ordinary folk whose taste is beyond comprehension, this little piece of *total and utter pre-pubescent shite* is going to go number one'. [*Beat.*] And it did.

SIDNEY: [*roaring*] *Will you shut up? Will you just shut up, Alfie? Will you try for just a moment to halt your descent into complete banality?* [*Beat.*] *There is more to life than rock and roll, Alfie.* [*Softly, fragile, breaking*] *I have to have this baby. I have to have this baby. I've got to have this baby. I have to have this baby. I have to have this baby. I have to have this baby.*

SCENE TWENTY-THREE

Night time. SIDNEY *is lying in subdued darkness.* JULIA *enters.*

JULIA: Did you eat?

SIDNEY: Esme made me something from the national cuisine of TransFat.

JULIA *sits down on a chair. Beat.*

JULIA: You can't let it matter that much.

SIDNEY: You can say that? After all this?

JULIA: Yes. Because in my own way—

SIDNEY: Oh, yes, yes! Oh yes.

JULIA: I do, Sidney—

SIDNEY: Oh, yes, you 'love' me. Yes, sure.

JULIA: Well, I—

SIDNEY: So easily invoked that word. By people who want to seem charitable or nice when they're just not. Okay, right, alright, you 'love' me because you're such a generous, 'big picture' kind of person—

JULIA: Actually, I was going to say, I like you.

Beat.

SIDNEY: Oh.

JULIA: I don't love you, Sidney.

SIDNEY: [*defensively*] I know that!

JULIA: I don't love very many people—

SIDNEY: And if I doubled your salary, Jules?

JULIA: I'd certainly try to love you a bit more.

SIDNEY: It's just extraordinary how you get away with stuff like that.

JULIA: Because when all around me I am surrounded by narcissism and panic, I keep my head. That's why you pay me, Sidney, even though I'm not that nice to you, because if I didn't keep my head, you'd lose yours.

SIDNEY: Thanks for the vote of confidence, Julia.

JULIA: Let her go.

SIDNEY: It's easy for you to say that.

JULIA: Is it?

SIDNEY: *You don't know what it is to want a baby.*

JULIA: You think I don't know what it is—?

SIDNEY: Not exactly, no. It's not instinctual to you, all right? I know that's not very PC or anything, but that's what I believe.

JULIA: You're entitled to your opinion.

SIDNEY: You hold me in contempt, don't you, Julia?

JULIA: Only in the way old married couples hold one another in contempt. When there's no—mystery.

SIDNEY: Alright then, I'm glad we've sorted that out. The point is, you'll never understand what I'm feeling because it's not part of who you are.

JULIA: Okay. [*She gets up. She starts to walk out then stops and turns around.*] Oh, by the way, I'm pregnant.

Beat.

SIDNEY: What? [*Beat.*] You're—?

JULIA: Yes.

Beat.

SIDNEY: You can't be!

JULIA: It's very early days.

SIDNEY: You're pregnant?

JULIA: Uh-huh.

SIDNEY: Really?

JULIA: Apparently.

Beat.

SIDNEY: [*slowly erupting*] That is— [*Beat.*] That is— [*Beat.*] *That is just wrong, Julia*. That is completely and utterly—That is just—That's just—*There is no God*. Admit it. There is no God or if there is, he is just an outright sadist. He's fat and he's never had a girlfriend and he lives in an old flat eating frozen pizza with a huge cosmic noticeboard thinking up devious fucking cruelties to bestow on *me*. Oh, he knuckles down to finetune the big ones: Darfur, Chinese earthquakes. Global pandemics. And then when he's a bit bored, he thinks: 'What the hell have I got to dump on Sidney Jones, a *very, very nice person* who wants nothing more than a teeny tiny egg to fertilise?' *What have I done?* What have I done in my life to evoke such karma? Jules. Jules, I'm asking you. What have I done that I should be punished and you—you of *all* people—*you* should be blessed?

JULIA: I'm—I'm sorry, Sidney.

SIDNEY: *Sorry!* As if *that's* going to make a difference! As if some kind of lame apology is going to impregnate me and absolve the complete and utter injustice. *Sorry!* Oh, I'm glad you're 'sorry'—thank you so bloody much for that, Julia.

JULIA: I really am, Sidney.

Beat. SIDNEY *calms down.*

SIDNEY: I'm—

JULIA: Go on—

SIDNEY: I'm—

JULIA: I can take it—

SIDNEY: I'm… *awash in irony*. [*Beat.*] Who's the father?

JULIA: I could tell you but then I'd have to kill you.

SIDNEY: Will the baby know?

JULIA: Probably not.

SIDNEY: It's not natural.

JULIA: Yes, but unnatural's the new natural.

SIDNEY: Are you resigning?

JULIA: If you want me to.

SIDNEY: I want you to!

JULIA: Okay. [*Beat.*] Do you want me to?

SIDNEY: Of course I don't want you to!

JULIA: I wasn't planning to.

SIDNEY: What? You're going to bounce around the world with me, with an infant in one of those horrible Norwegian slings?

JULIA: I won't work the first few months. I'll train a temp. After that, Midge will take over the baby.

SIDNEY: Don't be ridiculous!

JULIA: She's going to be a wonderful mother.

SIDNEY: The physique of Gerard Depardieu and the personality of Stalin. Not exactly Mary Poppins.

JULIA: A wonderful, caring mother.

SIDNEY: Jesus, Julia. Do you know what you're doing?

JULIA: Not entirely.

Beat.

SIDNEY: [*not vamping*] Those stories. About loonies. In shopping malls. Seeing a baby and just snatching it. Running. When I hear those stories, it's the *authorities* who seem mad to me. The snatcher—she seems completely and utterly *rational*.

JULIA: Sidney—

SIDNEY: Once you think you're never going to have a baby, the completely ordinary thought is 'How do I steal one?'

JULIA: Sidney—

SIDNEY: If you don't like it, can I have it?

SCENE TWENTY-FOUR

JULIA *and* ESME.

JULIA: I'm worried about her.
ESME: She's survived worse.
JULIA: She loves that baby, Esme.
ESME: Huh!

Beat.

JULIA: What?
ESME: No-one cares what I think. I'm old.
JULIA: I care.
ESME: I'm a foreigner, that's how it is when you cross over into old age—you're a foreigner. It's all a bit strange and you can't really complain too much because the place isn't designed for you—
JULIA: The place?
ESME: All of it.
JULIA: Here?
ESME: The whole thing. The planet.
JULIA: The planet's not designed for you?
ESME: The world's designed for thirty-year-olds, Julia. I'm over.
JULIA: You're not over, Esme.
ESME: I look around me and I don't recognise a thing. It's like being the only sober one at a party.
JULIA: The world's throwing a party and you're not invited.
ESME: And that's a good thing, because I wouldn't know what to wear, I wouldn't be able to hear anyone, there's no-one at the party I want to talk to anyway.
JULIA: This is your world, Esme.
ESME: No, Julia, it's not. And I don't want it to be. [*Beat.*] Sidney shouldn't get that baby.
JULIA: You don't think—?
ESME: Do you?
JULIA: I—I—I don't know.

ESME: These days everything's about us, isn't it? It's all about us and our rights and our needs and what's right and what's fair. And with all this adjudicating, all this measuring of what we are due, are we happier? Worrying about *ourselves* all the time?

JULIA: We—want things, Esme. Is it wrong to want things?

ESME: It's really not Sidney or me or you I'm worried about, Julia. It's the sheer belligerence of women's wishes that frightens me.

JULIA: You put me in that same boat as her, heh, Esme? [*Beat.*] At least have the *guts*—

ESME: I don't think two women should have children just because they can.

JULIA: It's not just because we can, Esme. It's because we can and *we want to*.

ESME: Children have the right to a mother and father who help them into themselves in an atmosphere of love.

JULIA: But not very many *straight* couples do that.

ESME: I think you should behave the way women like you have done for centuries—you have your friendships, but don't shout *look at me, look at me* and start raising babies just because modern life has brains but no taste.

JULIA: [*shocked*] What? Esme, I—I—

ESME: Children need a mother and a father and if the father sometimes loses his temper or the mother hits the gin, if they occasionally box their children's ears or forget to cuddle them at night, that's okay. That's actually better, Julia, than having two women raising them who tell them that the man embedded in their DNA is an irrelevancy and that *you can grow up to be God*. Those little Theas and Satchmos deserve to have their lousy, balding, insensitive, sexist fathers pushing their goddamn swings and nursing their disasters, not just on a register in a filing cabinet. Human beings have completely lost the sense of ordinary limits.

JULIA: Ordinary limits? Jesus, Esme— [*Uncharacteristically impassioned*] I think incredible, clever, extraordinary women have been stymied, silenced, sexualised and ignored for a very long time.

And after several thousand years of servitude, I don't really think that forty or so years of comparative freedom is quite enough to expunge the debt that is owed. I haven't had my fill. I want to put myself first for a bit longer. I want to explore every last desire. I want to chase every ambition. I want to give every tiny flicker of longing a serious chance to be requited and if that means bending the rules, fine by me. If we didn't adapt, Esme, we'd still be in the swamp. We'd still be swimming around without a backbone. It's civilisation, isn't it? Isn't it? Making families in different ways is not that much different to Mozart composing *The Magic Flute* or Tolstoy writing *Anna Karenina*. That's what we humans do. *We improve on nature.*

ESME: [*quietly*] Improve?

JULIA: You wanted a child, didn't you?

ESME: Yes, I did.

JULIA: And you never had one?

ESME: No, I couldn't. What we are *denied* gives us form. What we lose or never have—our disappointments and absences—these are the things that shape us. *We become what we are denied.*

SCENE TWENTY-FIVE

JULIA *and* SIDNEY *are in conversation.* JOLYON *is seated at some distance, reading the newspaper.*

SIDNEY: Well, what's the surname going to be?

JULIA: Mine's too boring. So we'll probably go with Midge's.

SIDNEY: Which is…?

JULIA: Geronimo.

SIDNEY: Geronimo.

JULIA: Yes.

SIDNEY: That's an actual surname?

JULIA: It's actually a fifteenth-century Tuscan aristocratic name.

SIDNEY: A barbarian name, then?

JULIA: [*stoically*] No, not barbarian.

SIDNEY: Well, it's… unusual.

JULIA: Well, I'm used to it, obviously.

SIDNEY: It's funny, I don't know why, but when I think of Midge, I think of her on the end of a battering ram.

JULIA: Do you think about her often, Sidney?

SIDNEY: So, if it's a girl?

JULIA: We'll probably go with… Plath or Arbus.

Beat.

SIDNEY: [*neutral*] Plath or Arbus?

JULIA: [*defensively*] Good, strong names evoking the world of female creativity.

SIDNEY: Oh, right.

JULIA: We don't want anything too run-of-the-mill. Something special.

SIDNEY: That's lovely, Jules. An 'homage' to the poet who stuck her head in the oven or the freaky photographer who slashed her wrists. She could go to kinder with little Van Gogh or Cobain.

JULIA: I think Arbus Geronimo is rather distinguished.

SIDNEY: Sure. If you want her confused with a Honda hatchback.

JULIA: We quite like [*suddenly doubting*] … Fig.

SIDNEY: Fig?

JULIA: Like the fruit.

SIDNEY: Oh, good idea.

JULIA: Well, Gwyneth had Apple.

SIDNEY: Why stop at fruit? Why not: Witlof Geronimo. That's 'special'.

JULIA: Why do you have to belittle me, Sidney? The moment I exercise any independent viewpoint—

SIDNEY: Right now you might think naming your child after produce is very cute but you'll wake up one day and think 'We must have been out of our minds'.

JULIA: Well, in any case, we're not going to decide until we see what she looks like.

SIDNEY: Oh, that's just bollocks, Julia. They're all the same when they come out. Small, red, wrinkly and ugly and any mother who says different is lying through her teeth.

JULIA: [*on her high horse*] Well, I beg to differ, Sidney. Actually. I think they come out with personalities fully formed. That tiny little creature is completely predestined to… to… love raspberry muffins and… and… hate— [*before she can stop herself*] curtains.

Beat. JULIA *looks utterly stricken.* JOLYON *slowly lowers the newspaper.* SIDNEY *is oblivious. An awful dawning on* JOLYON*'s face.*

SIDNEY: [*baffled*] Curtains?

JULIA: *Skirtings*. I said 'skirting boards'. The way some people really, *really* hate skirtings.

SIDNEY, *confused, moves on.*

SIDNEY: And if it's a boy?

JULIA: [*very disconcerted but trying to manage*] Well, actually, we quite like 'Alfie'.

SIDNEY: Oh, good idea. Brilliant role model. And every year, on his birthday, he will receive a hundred grams of coke from Uncle Alfie.

SCENE TWENTY-SIX

Very soon after. JOLYON *and* JULIA. *Very lively:*

JOLYON: *You set me up, Jules!*

JULIA: *Didn't you want to?*

JOLYON: Well…

JULIA: Did I force you to? Huh? Did I handcuff you to the bedhead?

JOLYON: [*genuinely unsure and unsettled*] I don't know. Did you?

JULIA: No-one will ever know it's you, Jolyon.

JOLYON: [*discovering*] *You wanted to get pregnant*. That was the entire reason you did it. You weren't overcome with lust!

JULIA: To be honest, Jol, no…

JOLYON: I'm wounded.

JULIA: You should be flattered. *I chose you*.

JOLYON: [*slightly mollified*] True.

JULIA: Of everyone. I chose *you*.

JOLYON: True. [*Touched, fishing*] Why me?

JULIA: I like you. Underneath everything, you're kind-hearted, you're not bad-looking and you were readily available.

JOLYON: What's that supposed to mean? 'Underneath everything'?

JULIA: Be happy for me, Jol.

JOLYON: I don't want a kid, Jules. Call me selfish, but I don't want to stand around in playgrounds fishing teeny peanut butter sandwiches out of Tupperware. I don't want to visit paedophile Santas in department stores or go to anything 'on ice'.

JULIA: I'm sure you'd like *Das Boot on Ice*, Jules.

JOLYON: [*alert*] Ooh! When's that on?

JULIA: Sidney doesn't have to know. No-one does. And I'll never mention it again. [*Beat.*] Jol?

He's mellowing.

We don't want a father. We don't actually need one.

JOLYON: Jeez, Jules, the world's moving too fast for me. Once upon a time you girls were secretaries not Secretaries of State. Now, you're out there running your multinationals, having your babies by yourselves in space shuttles and where are we in all this?

JULIA: You accept, Jol. You accept that while most women can seize forty minutes to feed a family of six, respond to twenty emails and write a screenplay, men are very sweetly trying to find the honey at the back of the fridge without moving anything. It's not your fault, Jol. It's the way you're programmed. And we keep you around for your one saving grace, the one thing that stops your sex from being a complete and total irrelevancy: the Y chromosome. That's your biological bodyguard. You know why it's called the 'Y' chromosome, don't you, Jol?

JOLYON: No, I don't.

JULIA: Because women said to God, '*Why* the hell didn't you give us that too?'

JOLYON: [*impressed*] I never knew that.

SCENE TWENTY-SEVEN

SIDNEY *and* TOBIAS. *High tension.*

TOBIAS: I've only got ten minutes.
SIDNEY: What did you say to her?
TOBIAS: She's a big girl. She can make up her own mind.
SIDNEY: What did you say to her?
TOBIAS: I told her to be alert to her responsibility.
SIDNEY: Responsibility to what?
TOBIAS: To the children, Sidney.
SIDNEY: Don't you think I think about the children? Don't you think when I close my eyes at night, that's what I see?
TOBIAS: *The children have no voice.*

Beat.

SIDNEY: What gives you the right to stand in judgement of me?
TOBIAS: [*steely*] I think we should all be standing in judgement of each other. I think we should scrutinise each other and welcome scrutiny. I think we'd have a better world if we stopped respecting each other's selfish choices because someone might look into *our* glasshouse and start throwing stones. I say, *'Throw the fucking stones'*. Let me fucking dodge them. Let me throw them back. But that's just me. [*Beat.*] There's a Rilke poem. 'Who shows a child, just as they are? Who sets it in its constellation and puts the measure of distance into its hand?'
SIDNEY: Jesus! We're surrounded by hatred and division and fear—
TOBIAS: [*wearily*] Oh, Sidney, what the fuck would you know?
SIDNEY: *I do fucking know*. This world is filled with hate. I have the capacity to *love* across difference. And so does she. [*Beat.*] If I don't take her, what's going to happen to her?
TOBIAS: I'm not a prophet.
SIDNEY: She'll die.
TOBIAS: She might die.
SIDNEY: And you think that's better?
TOBIAS: It's not about the baby.

SIDNEY: What?

TOBIAS: It's not about the baby.

SIDNEY: I think it *is* about the baby.

TOBIAS: It's about Africa.

SIDNEY: *I can't fix Africa.*

TOBIAS: No. Africa has to fix itself.

SIDNEY: And you can say that, can you? With your Cambridge education? You've got the *authority?*

TOBIAS: Theroux said the relief workers in Malawi reminded him of 'people herding animals and throwing food to them' like rangers in game parks.

SIDNEY: Jesus Christ! You're a Cambridge graduate with rich white parents. Do you represent your people any better than I do?

TOBIAS: *You're* the reason they're dying. With your baby snatching. *You guilty, rich, nice people are the ones who are killing us*!

SIDNEY: Doesn't she have the right to survive for long enough to decide *for herself* if she's first of all a human being, or first of all African? *That's her right.*

TOBIAS: [*unmistakably personal*] You think we're going to give you our future and be *grateful* to you?

Beat as SIDNEY *takes it in.*

SIDNEY: [*dawning on her*] You—*you*—

TOBIAS: *No-one ever asked me.*

Long beat.

SIDNEY: She could die.

TOBIAS: She could die. But she might not. She might become a supermodel or a federal judge. It happens. Or she could live here, and be a shadow.

SIDNEY: [*furious*] Is that what you are? Are you a shadow? Successful journalist, drinking in pubs, bedding girls, reading Ian McEwen, listening to Radiohead… What? Not a life worth having? Don't you think you got lucky?

TOBIAS: Well, we'll never know, will we? If I got lucky.

SIDNEY: Did you ever think that asking that question might be a gift in itself? Someone thought you'd be better off if you were loved.

TOBIAS: I'm just not altogether convinced, Sidney. That if you're stolen to be loved, the loving really counts.

Long beat.

SIDNEY: You're not African. Anymore.

TOBIAS: No. No, you're right. And one day she'll be standing here, just like me. It will all lead to this moment. Right here. When she's thirty years old and standing in front of you saying, *'It wasn't Cambridge I wanted. It was someone to show me the measure of distance.'*

SIDNEY: *I'll* show her the measure of distance.

TOBIAS: But, Sidney, you'll never know the distance she's travelled.

SCENE TWENTY-EIGHT

TOBIAS *and* LAYLA.

TOBIAS: Coming back?

LAYLA: Thinking about it.

TOBIAS: I know you will.

LAYLA: I do have a deep-seated attraction to the concept of reform.

He smiles.

TOBIAS: You're not going to sign, are you?

Beat.

LAYLA: What happens if I do?

Silence.

TOBIAS: There's no point in asking that.

LAYLA: I want to know. What happens if I sign the form?

Long beat.

TOBIAS: [*resolving*] Then don't come back for my sake.

Silence.

LAYLA: My God. My God!

TOBIAS: *You can't do it*. You can't look at me, you can't talk to me, *you can't love me* and repeat the same mistake. *Don't give her the baby. Don't tell the world if you're rich and white you can get anything you like, including flesh and blood. Don't let people like Sidney take a little bit of Africa instead of helping Africa take care of its own. Don't turn your brothers and sisters into currency. Don't turn babies into rewards for being born lucky. Find another way.*

LAYLA: And if she dies?

TOBIAS: She dies.

LAYLA: You don't know how to feel.

TOBIAS: You don't know how to feel what I feel.

LAYLA: You think the truth is everything.

TOBIAS: What's more important than the truth?

Beat.

LAYLA: Hope.

He moves to touch her. She draws away.

What if she's my father's child?

Beat.

TOBIAS: [*stunned*] *What?*

LAYLA: The baby.

TOBIAS: But she's not. [*He thinks.*] Layla? She's not. Is she?

LAYLA: What if her mother was the maid? What if my father got her pregnant, because he's a bastard and she was nineteen years old and intimidated and wanted to keep her job because she's the only one in her family earning a decent wage? What if a few months after the birth, her mother dies and my father allows the child to go to an orphanage, because he's weak, and even though he sings hymns in church, his higher church is pragmatism?

TOBIAS: Jesus.

LAYLA: *What if she's my sister?*

Long beat.

TOBIAS: That would—

LAYLA: What—?

TOBIAS: Well—

LAYLA: So—?

TOBIAS: That—that—

Long beat.

LAYLA: [*quietly*] The only way to live in Africa is to be buried in it, so you can't see it. But I've lived one foot in Africa and one foot out and I *can* see it. When the *chiperoni*—the drifting mist—clears, I can see the ugliness of the savannah with the shanty huts, the pathetic maize crops ruined by floods, the schools emptied of books by thieves, the beggars who never ask for work, only for money. There are times I look up and in a second, without even realising, I'm thinking: *'It's not worth saving'*. Let the continent be swallowed up by the earth. Let it fall into the sea. Let there be dark blue water from the southern tip of Malta to the northern edge of the Antarctic.

He tries to hold her. She resists.

It's the ambivalence in *us*, that's the problem. *We're* the problem.

TOBIAS: Layla—

LAYLA: She's there, isn't she? Right there in front of you. Those soft brown eyes, that tiny face. Expression there, a tiny frown between the eyebrows, a ghostly look of something wise or worried flitting across her face like a cloud, a stretch of hand. Easy to invest in. A connection. Makes her real. And now she's *connected*, you want to save her.

TOBIAS: Layla—

LAYLA: And what about the baby lying next to her? That *other* baby. And the one next to her? And the one next to him?

Silence.

TOBIAS: [*realising*] She's not, is she?

Beat.

LAYLA: She could have been.

SCENE TWENTY-NINE

A park. Blue sky. LAYLA *sits on a bench. She holds the blue form and a pen. She is thinking.* SIDNEY *sees her from a distance. She watches her for a few moments before approaching her and sitting down.*

LAYLA: In the village where I'm from, there are piles of steel mounting up on the edges of town. Computers. For years, the West has been sending container loads of computer equipment. We're a junkyard for your compassion. Are computers going to save Africa? Growing hills of steel? It's not computers we need. It's imagination. Can you send us that? We need to see Africa as it might be, but *there's no-one left to imagine.*

LAYLA *stares at the blue form. She picks up the pen. Puts it down. Picks it up again.*

SIDNEY: This doesn't have to be about everything. It can just be about us.

Beat.

LAYLA: But who is 'us'?

SIDNEY *stands. She walks a small distance, turns and watches her for a moment, then turns and walks away. Long beat.* LAYLA *picks up the pen, it hovers.*

Light diminishes on her and simultaneously comes up on the original makeshift bassinet. Again, the soundscape is growing louder: tiny snatches of African music, crying, laughter, a mother singing a lullaby, traffic noises, animal noises, babies crying, soothing words, airplane noises, snatches of conversation, lullabies, TV, radio—a chaotic but somehow rhythmically beautiful jumble of culturally diverse sounds, stolen from a life.

At the crescendo: blackout.

THE END

JOANNA MURRAY-SMITH's plays have been produced throughout Australia and all over the world, including *Honour* which had a public reading with Meryl Streep and was produced on Broadway in 1998, the National Theatre, London, in 2003, and on the West End with Dame Diana Rigg in 2005. Other plays include *Ninety*, *Bombshells*, *Rapture*, *Nightfall*, *Redemption*, *Love Child*, *Atlanta* and *Flame*, many of which have been translated into other languages and adapted for radio. In 2008 her play *The Female of the Species* was produced on the West End. The same year her adaptation of Bergman's *Scenes from a Marriage* was directed by Sir Trevor Nunn in 2008 at the Belgrade Theatre, Coventry. She has won many awards, including the Victorian Premier's Award for Best New Play (*Honour* and *Rapture*) and in 2008 *The Female of the Species* was nominated for an Olivier Award. Her novels include *Truce* (1994), *Judgement Rock* (2002), both published by Penguin Australia and *Sunnyside* (2005), published by Penguin Australia and Viking in the UK. She lives in Melbourne with her husband and three children.